From Bath Chaps to Bara Brith

The Taste of South West Britain

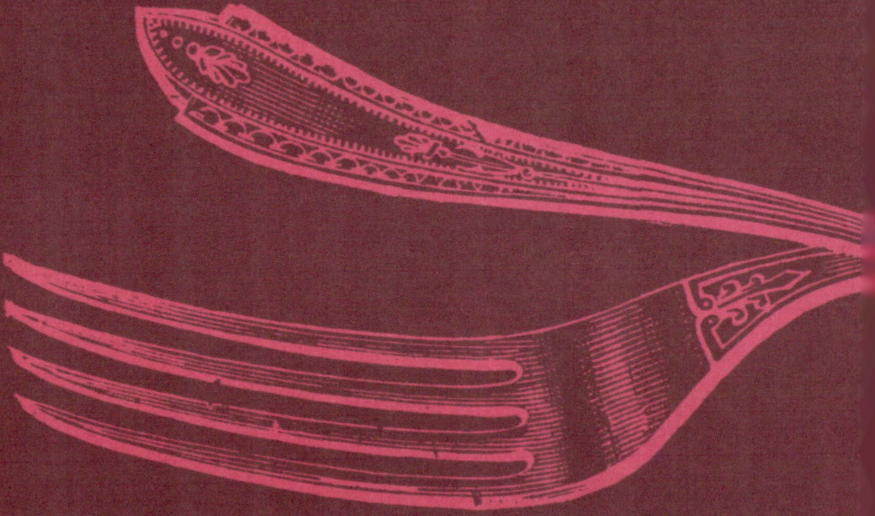

From Bath Chaps to Bara Brith

The Taste of South-West Britain

Laura Mason and Catherine Brown

Foreword by Hugh Fearnley-Whittingstall

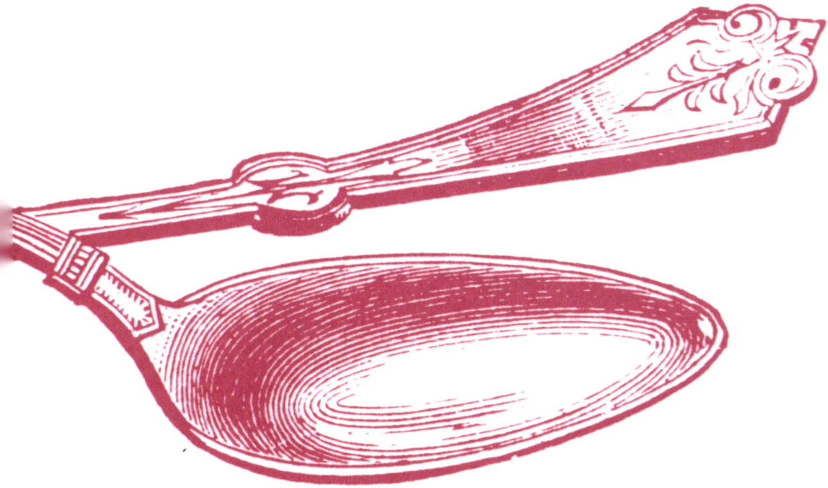

Harper Press
An imprint of HarperCollins*Publishers*

Harper*Press*
An imprint of HarperCollins*Publishers*
77–85 Fulham Palace Road
Hammersmith, London W6 8JB
www.harpercollins.co.uk

Published by Harper Press in 2007

First published in Great Britain in 1999
as part of *Traditional Foods of Britain*
by Prospect Books
Allaleigh House, Blackawton, Totnes, Devon TQ9 7DL

Subsequently published by Harper*Press* in 2006 as part of *The Taste of Britain*
Original design by **'OMEDESIGN**

9 8 7 6 5 4 3 2 1

A catalogue record for this book
is available from the British Library

ISBN: 978-0-00-726785-9

Design by Envy Design Ltd

Printed and bound in China

From Bath Chaps to Bara Brith is part of a series of books about regional British food which include:

Bedfordshire Clangers and Lardy Cake
Traditional Foods from the South and South East

From Norfolk Knobs to Fidget Pie
Foods from the Heart of England and East Anglia

From Eccles Cake to Hawkshead Wig
A Celebration of Northern Food

From Petticoat Tails to Arbroath Smokies
Traditional Foods of Scotland

These books originally formed part of the complete volume, *The Taste of Britain*, published by Harper*Press* in 2006.

Contents

Foreword

Much is made these days of British food culture. Chefs and food writers, myself included, are keen to tell you that it's thriving, it should be celebrated, it's as good as anything our Continental cousins enjoy. Yet sometimes it seems as if our words come rolling back to us, as if bouncing off some distant landmass, unheard and unheeded along the way, so that we begin to have trouble persuading ourselves, let alone others, that there is something here worth fighting for.

The fact is that if you spend much time in supermarkets, or amongst the proliferation of branded fast foods on any high street, or if you eat in any but a handful of UK restaurants or pubs, then the concept of regional British food can seem a bit like Father Christmas, or Nirvana. A lovely romantic idea, but it doesn't really exist, does it?

Well, yes, it does. And if you're having trouble finding it, it may just be because you are looking in the wrong place. The problem, in part at least, is that the best, most uplifting stories about British food culture are being drowned out by the cacophony of mediocrity, and worse. The Turkey Twizzler is front page news – and rightly so, when it is making pre-basted, additive-laced butterballs of our children themselves. Shavings of Turkey 'ham' – 98 per cent fat free, of course – are filling the sandwiches of figure-conscious office workers the length and breadth of the nation. But the Norfolk Black, a real turkey slow-grown and bred for flavour, is out there, too – waiting to show you what he's worth. He's not making a song and dance – just gobbling quietly to himself. Track him down, and you're in for a revelation.

That's why this series of books are so timely, so necessary – and so brilliantly useful. They are a map, an investigative tool that will enable you to leave behind the homogenous and the bland, and set off on an exciting journey to find Britain's edible treasure – some of which may turn out to be hidden on your very doorstep.

I urge you not merely to browse them, but to use them. Because if you can get out there and discover for yourself some of our great British specialities – whether it's traditional sage Derby cheese, or the Yorkshire teacakes known as Fat Rascals, or a properly aged Suffolk cider vinegar – then you will discover, or at least remind yourself, that food can be so much more than fuel. That it can, several times a day, every day of our lives, relax us, stimulate us, and give us pleasure.

The foods described in this book can all work that small daily miracle of exciting our passions. Not all of them, for all of us. But each of them for some of us. They have been made and honed over generations – sometimes centuries – and they are still with us because enough of us – sometimes only just enough of us – love them. Of course, in many instances, we have yet to discover whether we love them or not. And that is why this book is so loaded with fantastic potential. Everybody has a new favourite food waiting for them in the pages ahead.

I've travelled fairly widely, if somewhat randomly, around Britain, and tracking down and tasting local foods has become an increasing priority for me. Very uplifting it is, too. Approach our regional food culture with a true sense of curiosity, and you can never become an old hand, or a jaded palate. I still feel a great sense of excitement and discovery when I finally get to eat a classic local dish on its own home turf. You can't easily deconstruct the magic formula of a well-made Lancashire Hot Pot, or a Dorset apple cake. It is in the nature of such dishes that their sum is greater than their parts. But you can, when you find a version that hits the spot, instantly appreciate how such dishes have survived the harsh natural selection of public taste, and come to delight, comfort and sustain families and groups of friends for so long.

Recently, for instance, I managed to track down my very first proper Yorkshire curd tart, its delectable filling made from colostrum – the very rich milk produced by a cow for her newborn calf. It was baked for me by a farmer's wife at home in her own kitchen, using the method passed down to her through her family, and it was wonderful – very rich, curdy and slightly crumbly – having a hint of cakiness without the flouriness (I told you deconstruction was a vain enterprise). Anyway, it was a world away from any 'regular' custard tart I'd tried before. What I learnt from that experience, and from many similar ones, is that regionality really does matter. If that tart had been made in Dorset or in the Highlands, it wouldn't have tasted the same. And if it had not been made at all, the world – and on that drizzly autumn day, me – would have been the poorer for it.

There are so many factors that affect the way a food turns out. Cheese is the best example. I love cheese – 'milk's leap toward immortality' as someone once said – and it never ceases to amaze me. It's made from milk, of course, plus something that will make the milk curdle (usually rennet, but sometimes quirkier coagulants, like nettle juice). Two basic ingredients. Yet cheese is one of the most diverse foods known to man. There are hundreds of varieties in the British Isles alone – and a bowlful of fresh, pillowy Scottish crowdie differs so greatly from a nutty Somerset cheddar that it's hard to believe they're basically the same stuff. The breed of cattle and their diet, the local water and pasture, the yeasts and bacteria that live locally in the air, the techniques used to curdle the milk, the way the cheese is pressed, turned, and aged – all these things affect the outcome.

That's why it seems absolutely right to me that only cheese made in a handful of Midlands dairies can be called Stilton, and that beer brewed with the gypsum-rich water in Burton-upon-Trent is labelled as such. What's more, if you understand why regional products are unique – that it's high temperatures and seaweed fertiliser that make Jersey Royals taste different to any other potatoes, for instance – then you know more about food in general. An understanding of regional diversity can only make us more intelligent and appreciative eaters.

This understanding is not always easy to come by. Most other European countries have long taken for granted that local foods should be protected, their unique identity preserved. Hence the French

AOC and the Italian DOC systems. But it's an idea not everyone in this country is comfortable with. I put this down to two things, and the first is the creeping curse of supermarket culture. The big multiple retailers try to tell us that we can eat whatever we want, whenever we want and indeed wherever we want. If you understand the seasonal nature of fresh produce, you know this is neither true nor desirable – and the same goes for regionality. You might not be able to buy genuine Arbroath smokies in every shop in the land, but that is precisely what makes them special when you do find them.

The second reason for resistance to regional labelling is illustrated by the pork pie issue. The pie makers of Melton Mowbray are currently battling to have their product awarded PGI (Protected Geographic Indication) status. That would mean only pies made in the area, to a traditional recipe, could carry the name. Other pork pie makers, from other areas, object to this. They want to call their products Melton Mowbray pies, too, arguing that their recipe is much the same. That's nonsense, of course: a recipe is only the beginning of a dish, a mere framework. The where, the how and the who of its making are just as important. But why would you even want to call your pie a Mowbray pie if it comes from London, or Swansea? Only, perhaps, if you know the real Mowbray pies taste better, and you can't be bothered to make your own recipe good enough to compete.

All of which goes to show why the issue of regionality is as relevant today as it ever has been. It's important not to see *From Bath Chaps to Bara Brith* as a history book, a compendium of nostalgic culinary whimsy. The food included here is alive and well, and there is nothing described in these pages that you can't eat today, as long as you go to the right place. That's perhaps the most important criterion for inclusion because our regional food traditions are just as much part of the future as the past. At least, they had better be, or we will be in serious trouble.

The implications for our health, and the health of our environment, are far-reaching. If we eat, say, fruit that's produced locally, not only do we reduce the food miles that are wrecking our climate, but that fruit will be fresher and richer in nutrients. If we can go to a butcher's shop to buy meat that's been raised nearby, we can ask the butcher how it was farmed, and how it was slaughtered. And perhaps we can take our children with us, so they learn something too. In the end, a local food culture, supplied in the main by contiguous communities, militates against secrecy, adulteration – cruelty even – and in favour of transparency, accountability and good practice. What could be more reassuring than knowing the names and addresses of the people who produce your food?

I don't think it's overstating the case, either, to say that a knowledge of regional cooking promotes resourcefulness and a renewed respect for food in all of us. Regional dishes are, by their very nature, simple things. This is folk cooking – a 'nose to tail' approach that uses whatever's available and makes it go as far as possible. For a while now – since conspicuous consumption has become practically an end in itself – our predecessors' abhorrence of throwing away anything may have seemed at best, quaint, at worst, laughable. But as we begin to come to terms with the consequences of our 'have it all now' culture, it is becoming clear that ethical production, good husbandry, environmental responsibility and kitchen thrift all go hand in hand. The frugal culture that gave birth to chitterlings and lardy cake, Bath chaps and bread pudding is something we should be proud to belong to. To re-embrace it can only do us good.

Aside from their currency, the foods in this book have had to prove themselves in other ways. They must be unique to a specific region and they must have longevity, having been made or produced for at least 75 years. Finally, they must be, to use a rather ugly word, 'artisanal'. That means that special knowledge and skills are required to make them properly. Which brings me to one crucial element of good food that should never be forgotten: the people who make it. Almost without exception, the brewers, bakers, cooks, farmers and fishermen who produce traditional foods are what you might call 'characters'. This doesn't mean they are yokels caught in a yesteryear time warp. They are people of passion and commitment, intelligence and good humour, and often extraordinary specialist knowledge. And they know more than most of us about the meaning of life.

Not a single one of them goes to work in the morning in order to make lots of money – you certainly don't choose to devote your life to bannock-making in the hope it will furnish you with a swimming pool and a Ferrari. They do it because they believe in it and, ultimately, feel it is worthwhile. In their own quiet and industrious way, they understand just how much is at stake. The future of civilized, communal, respectful life on our islands? It is not preposterous to suggest it. Use your regular custom and generously expressed enthusiasm to support this modest army of dedicated souls, working away in their kitchens, gardens, orchards breweries and smokehouses all over Britain, and you do a great deal more than simply save a cheese, or a beer, for posterity. You help save the next generation from the tyranny of industrial mediocrity.

Amid this talk of pride and principles, it's crucial not to lose sight of the fact that this is food to be enjoyed, celebrated – and shared with friends. Dishes don't survive down the centuries unless they taste good. You may not need much persuasion to try some of the buttery cakes or fabulously fresh fruit and veg described in these pages. But you will perhaps need a sense of adventure to rediscover the charms of some of the entries. Be ready to cast your squeamishness aside and sample some tripe, some tongue, some trotters as well. If the experience of visitors to our River Cottage events here in Dorset is anything to go by, I'm betting you'll be pleasantly surprised. You'll be taking a pig's head home from the butcher's and making your own brawn before you can say, 'Er, not for me, thanks.'

One element of this series of books to be richly savoured is the language. Originally published as part of the complete volume, *The Taste of Britain*, they are written by Laura Mason and Catherine Brown, without hyperbole, but with a precision and clarity that far better express their authors' underlying passion and purpose. Another thing that makes them a joy to read is their embrace of the regional food vernacular: Dorset knobs, Puggie Buns, Singin' Hinnnies, Black Bullets and Mendip Wallfish are all to be revelled in for their names alone. Indeed, some might be tempted to enjoy them as a glorious catalogue of eccentricity, a celebration of the cowsheel and the careless gooseberry, of the head cheese and the damson cheese (neither of which are actually cheese) that make British food so charming and idiosyncratic.

But to do so would be to miss out. Now that this book exists, now that it is in your hands, use it to bring about change. It should not be taken as a slice of the past, in aspic, but as a well-stocked store cupboard, with the potential to enrich our future food culture. See it not as a preservation order for British regional foods, but a call to action. Use this book as a guide, not merely to seek out delicious things that you've never tried before, but also to recreate some of them in your own kitchen. Do that and you'll be actively participating in a great food culture that has always been with us, that is often hidden beneath the mass-produced, homogenous, seasonless food we are so frequently offered, but which may yet have a vibrant future.

This book - along with the rest in the series - is a thorough and splendid answer to the question 'What is British food?' Use it well, and it may help to ensure that is still a meaningful question a hundred years from now.

Hugh Fearnley-Whittingstall

Preface

In 1994 we embarked on a mission to describe as many British foods with regional affiliations as we could find. We were part of a Europe-wide project working within a framework – handed down from Brussels – which demanded a link to the *terroir* (soil). In fact the project, named Euroterroir, was more suited to rural southern Europe than industrialized, urbanized Britain. How do you link Yorkshire Relish to the soil? But ultimately we succeeded in writing up some four hundred British entries. And along the way we asked some broader questions – what are our traditional foods? What is the character of British taste?

We've discovered that many rural treasures had survived against the odds. That sometimes foods with traditional or regional affiliations languished unloved. That sometimes British foods, though not always linking directly to the *terroir*, did have other powerful historical influences which made them special, and distinct, from the rest of Europe. No other country in Europe has a history of spicing to match the British.

Yet our homogenized food supply was clearly inflicting a far-reaching loss of local distinctiveness and quality. The idea, inherent in the project, that foods should be the property of a place and its community (*terroir*, in the context of food in France, carries implications of regionality, cultural groupings and the influence of trade and climate), rather than the trademarked possession of an individual or company, was especially alien.

Our initial research complete, we felt confident that either the Ministry of Agriculture or Food from Britain would take up the cause and publish a book based on the work which had taken us two years to complete. Instead, it was a small publisher in Devon (Tom Jaine of

Prospect Books) who kept the flag flying and *Traditional Foods of Britain* was published in 1999. Eight years on we welcome this series published by HarperCollins.

We also welcome signs of change. Now, there is more awareness of commercial dilution, and dishonest imitation and therefore the need to protect food names, though the application process for producers is slow and difficult. There are certainly more small producers working locally, but they have to cope with numerous barriers. However much they protest otherwise, powerful supermarket central distribution systems and cut-throat pricing polices are not designed to foster local produce. And consumers do not always pause to consider the more subtle and elusive nuances of foods from closer to home.

Of course the ties of regionality do not suit foodstuffs, and in any case should be just one of many avenues open to British farmers and food producers. But it would be good to see more raw local ingredients transformed into distinctive foods since records show their rich variety in the past. Shops and markets bursting with colourful and varied local produce are one of the great pleasures of shopping for food on the continent. They exist because national policies and local custom support them. They should not be impossible in Britain. These books are not an end but a beginning.

Laura Mason and Catherine Brown 2007

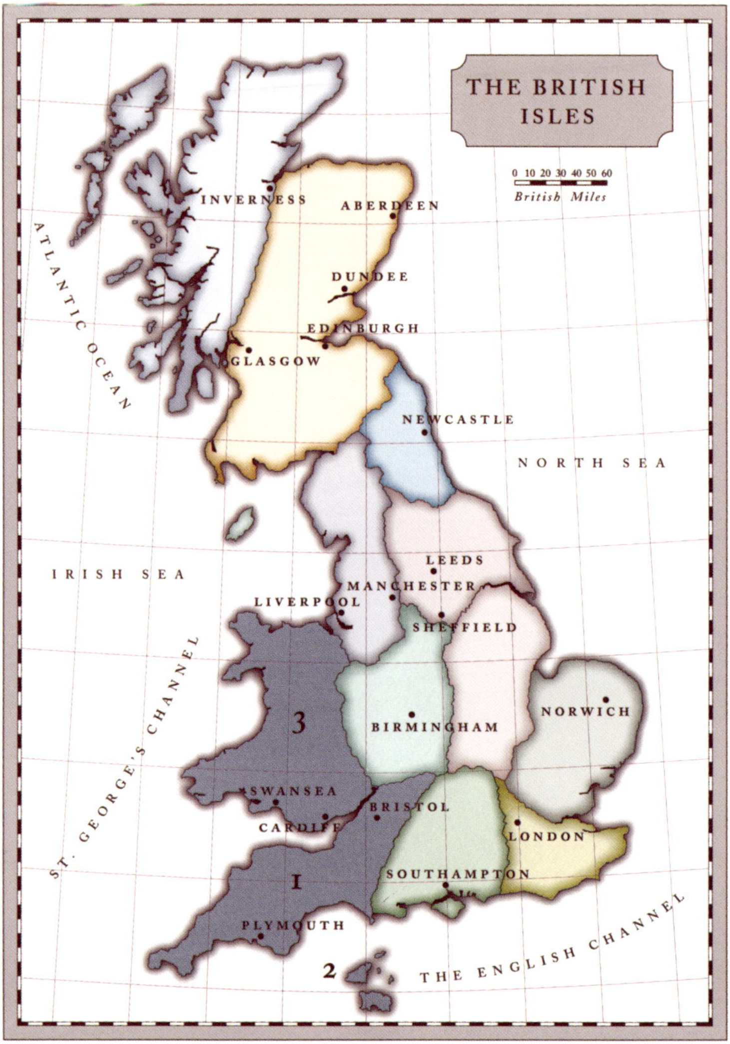
THE BRITISH ISLES
0 10 20 30 40 50 60
British Miles
INVERNESS
ABERDEEN
DUNDEE
EDINBURGH
GLASGOW
ATLANTIC OCEAN
NEWCASTLE
NORTH SEA
IRISH SEA
LEEDS
MANCHESTER
LIVERPOOL
SHEFFIELD
ST. GEORGE'S CHANNEL
NORWICH
3
BIRMINGHAM
SWANSEA
BRISTOL
CARDIFF
LONDON
SOUTHAMPTON
1
PLYMOUTH
2
THE ENGLISH CHANNEL

Regions

1. *South West England*

2. *Channel Islands*

3. *Wales*

South West England

Dittisham Plum

DESCRIPTION:

A medium-large red dessert plum, of oval-oblong shape; it has golden yellow flesh and an excellent rich flavour. The havest is very short, from the second to third weeks in August.

HISTORY:

This is a localized plum variety, grown in and around one village in Devon. It is sometimes known as the Dittisham Small Red and, locally, as the Dittisham Ploughman. It is a chance seedling, appreciated in the locality and propagated by suckers. This process is common to a number of plum varieties in England. The Kea in Cornwall is very like the Dittisham although smaller and with a slightly later season.

A number of myths luxuriate around the supposed origin of this plum: that they were grown from a cargo of fruit or from seedlings dumped by a ship, the villagers planting trees in their gardens; or that the original plum came from Holland or Germany, and that the name 'ploughman' is a corruption of the German for plum, *Pflaume*; or that the nuns of the Priory of Cornworthy, nearby, brought them to the district in centuries past. There is nothing to substantiate any of these beliefs.

Oral tradition is that before motor transport, people from towns as far away as Plymouth came by horse and cart (a journey of several hours) to collect large quantities of plums. The variety was received at the National Fruit Trials in 1949. A liqueur based on these plums is now available locally. The fruit is macerated in grain spirit.

TECHNIQUE:

Dittisham lies at sea level on the estuary of the River Dart, a wide, drowned valley which opens on to the south coast of Devon. The climate is mild and sheltered, protected from the north and west winds by high hills. The soil is slightly acid and shaley. Local people claim that this plum will not flourish anywhere but Dittisham. It is propagated from suckers, and most cottage gardens in the area contain an example. There are also orchards, which generally receive little attention except at fruiting time. Under normal circumstances, the plums flower and fruit without difficulty, but easterly winds during the flowering season may adversely affect the blossoms and, therefore, the crop.

REGION OF PRODUCTION:

SOUTH WEST ENGLAND.

Bath Cheese

DESCRIPTION:

UNPASTEURIZED, SOFT COW'S MILK CHEESE. DIMENSIONS: 8CM SQUARE, 2CM DEEP. WEIGHT: 250G. COLOUR: CREAM, WITH WHITE MOULD SURFACE. FLAVOUR AND TEXTURE: MILD, WITH SLIGHT ACID FLAVOUR, MELLOWING WITH AGE, CREAMY TEXTURE.

HISTORY:

Bath cheese is mentioned in several late-Victorian texts. *Law's Grocer's Manual* (*c.* 1895) said it was 'a noted kind of soft creamy cheese'. Conditions imposed upon farm cheese-makers during the first half of the twentieth century were unfavourable for the soft, moist category of cheese to which this belongs. It was not made for many years until the current maker revived it in the 1980s.

TECHNIQUE:

Unpasteurized milk from one herd of Friesian cattle is used. Starter is added to milk at about 32°C, then animal rennet, and it is allowed to coagulate. The curd is cut to encourage whey separation to begin, and the curds and whey ladled into moulds placed on rush mats. The cheeses stand overnight. The surface is dry-salted, after which the cheese is left to dry 2 days at about 15°C. It is ripened in cooler conditions for 3–4 weeks. The cheese is made all year but is best in the autumn.

REGION OF PRODUCTION:

South West England, Bath (Somerset).

Baydon Hill Cheese

DESCRIPTION:

An unpasteurized cow's and sheep's milk cheese. Weight: 2 sizes, the larger weighs about 2.3kg; the smaller about 450g. Form: the larer is a truckle (tall cylinder); the smaller is a round or loaf, as such cheeses are known locally. Colour: that of the cow's milk cheese is golden yellow; the sheep's milk version is a paler, buttery colour; both are waxed with natural beeswax. Flavour and teture: the cow's milk cheese is mild and creamy; the sheep's milk cheese is denser, with a sweet rich flavour.

HISTORY:

This is a modern version of a cheese formerly known as Wiltshire. Its history over the past 200 years is fairly well documented. It is related by method to Cheddar and Gloucester cheeses; as with the latter, both a thick and a thin version were known in the past. Val Cheke (1959) estimates that in 1798 5,000 tons of North Wiltshire cheese were made. This was said to be of excellent quality and in part was attriued to the particular method of dairying in Wiltshire which allowed for consistency in temperature and method. At this time, the milk of Longhorn cattle was used; these have long since been replaced by modern dairy breeds. As with Cheddar, there is some evidence for communal cheese-making. Small cheeses, known as Wiltshire loaves, and larger ones, similar to Gloucesters, are both recorded. A sheep's milk cheese is now made to the same recipe.

The local cheese-making industry declined rapidly after 1914–18 and remained a memory until Jo Hale, a farmer's wife, began her research in the late 1980s. She located a family recipe for North Wiltshire Cheese and has developed it for both sheep's and cow's milk under the name of Baydon Hill, where she lives.

TECHNIQUE:

The milk comes from a flock of British Friesland sheep, pastured in the valley of the River Avon, or from the maker's herd of cattle, mosly Friesians with a little Guernsey, feeding on semi-permanent ley pature. It is not pasteurized. The method is the same for both cheeses.

Starter is added, plus annatto, followed shortly afterwards by a vegetarian rennet, and the milk left for the curd to form. It is cut into cubes of roughly 1cm. The temperature is raised slightly and the curd stirred for about 100 minutes until the correct acidity is reached; then it is allowed to settle for a few minutes and the whey is drained off. The curd is cut in blocks and turned up to 5 times; the number of turns varies according to the state of the milk, and fewer turns may be required with the sheep's milk curd. The curd is milled, salted and put into moulds. It is pressed for about 2 days, the cheeses being turned once. The cheeses are removed from their moulds; the larger ones are larded and bandaged, the smaller ones simply larded. They are stored for 4 months, turned daily for the first 6 weeks and once a week thereafter; then they are washed, dried, waxed and distributed.

REGION OF PRODUCTION:

South West, Wiltshire.

Beenleigh Blue Cheese

DESCRIPTION:

There are 3 cheeses in this group: Devon Blue (cow's milk); Harbourne Blue (goat's milk), and Beenleigh Blue (sheep's milk). Dimensions: Beenleigh Blue: 14cm diameter, 12cm deep; Devon Blue: 16cm diameter, 12cm deep; Harbourne Blue: about 16cm diameter, 12cm deep. Weight: 2.5–3kg. Colour: Beenleigh Blue: very pale creamy yellow, with green-blue veining; Devon Blue: very pale cream, almost white, with pale green-grey veining; Harbourne Blue: almost white, with very slight green tint, grey-green veining. Flavour and texture: Beenleigh Blue,

RICH VELVETY TEXTURE, WELL-BALANCED FLAVOUR NOTES OF BLUE, SALT AND SHEEP, WITH UNDERLYING SWEETNESS; DEVON BLUE, FIRM TEXTURED AND SALTY, CARAMEL-LEATHER FLAVOUR NOTE; HARBOURNE BLUE, FIRM TEXTURE, INITIAL GOAT TANG, DEVELOPING INTO A RICH BLUE FLAVOUR.

HISTORY:

This cheese originated in the late 1970s in Devon. It arose in part from necessity, as the producer sought new markets for sheep's milk; one answer was to make a blue cheese. The person who developed Beenleigh Blue and its sister cheeses, Robin Congdon, was one of a handful of pioneers in the artisan manufacture of fine cheeses. This tradition, once vibrant in the British Isles, had almost died out duing the 1940s under the impact of strict rationing.

Sheep's milk cheese may once have been made in southern England – indeed, it was the dominant type – but Beenleigh Blue was the first blue sheep's milk cheese to be made in the area for many years. The milk comes from 2 flocks kept nearby the dairy. Devon Blue, made from milk of a designated herd not far distant, was developed in the mid-1980s; Harbourne Blue is a new addition to the range, made from goat's milk from a single farm on the edge of Dartmoor.

TECHNIQUE:

Beenleigh Blue: the milk is heat-treated for 30 minutes before cheese-making commences. Starter is added, followed by vegetarian rennet and a culture of *penicillium roquefortii*; the curd is left for about 45 minutes, the exact time depending on the season, as this affects the quality of the milk. After cutting, the curd is stirred gently, then allowed to settle for about 15 minutes. The curd is broken by hand and packed into moulds, in which it remains for 2 days. The cheese is surface-salted, spiked after a few days, allowed to blue, and then wrapped in foil to stop the rind. The cheese is matured for up to 6 months. The methods for making Devon and Harbourne are very similar, but the first is matured for about 3 months. Season: Beenleigh Blue, made January–July, available September–February; Devon Blue, all year; Harbourne Blue, made all year, but the largest quantities are produced in the spring and early summer.

REGION OF PRODUCTION:

South West England, Devon.

Cheddar Cheese

DESCRIPTION:

Pressed cow's milk cheese. Cheddar is produced in many different sizes weighing 500g–30kg. The traditional shape is a cylinder. Small ones are known as truckles. Cheddar cheeses were bandaged and smeared with lard to prevent the rind from cracking and to reduce evaporation, a practice which some producers still follow, although others now dip the cheeses in yellow wax. Rindless cheese, made by the Cheddar method in blocks of about 19kg, is now commonly available. Colour: good Cheddar is an even pale yellow. Flavour: depends on maturity. In general it is rich with a sharp note and a nutty aftertaste; sharpness strengthens with age. Some manufacturers offer smoked cheeses or add herbs.

HISTORY:

The name is taken from the village of Cheddar on the southern edge of the Mendips. Points to note are a long history, the apparently consistent excellence of the cheese, a cooperative system for its production, and the way in which the techniques associated with it have spread around the world, though often abused. The name may mislead, however. Although first-class in the parish of Cheddar itself, this cheese was from the outset made throughout the county and the wider region. The name, it is suggested, was attached to the cheese because the fame of Cheddar Gorge defined the district of origin.

Medieval records demonstrate that cheese-making was already undertaken in the region, but more precise information is not forthcoming until the modern period. In the seventeenth century, the communal pooling of milk to make very large truckles was a matter of remark, although few of them can have been as large as the cheese made for Lord Weymouth that 'was big enough to hold a girl of 13'. All the milk was contributed to a common dairy, or 'cheddar club' which meant each cheese could be much larger than those from small, individual herds, so making them fit for long maturing, which accounts for their excellent flavour. This set Cheddar cheese apart from much of the competition. Already, by 1662, they were 'so few and so dear [that they are] hardly to be met with, save at some great man's table' (Rance, 1982). The system was also sufficiently scouted to be hinted at in a play by Aphra Behn in the late seventeenth century. Its high reputation continued. Rance notes that in the early eighteenth century, Cheddar was described as 'the most noted place in England for making large, fine, rich and pleasant cheese' and that milk was brought into the common dairy and the quantities noted down in a book kept for the purpose. Profit from selling cheese was given back in proportion to the amount of milk each person contributed. Cooperative cheese-making continued until the First World War. Cheeses were indeed very large, weighing 90–120 pounds (45–60kg); cheeses of up to one and a half hundredweight (about 90kg) were noted in *Law's Grocer's Manual* in the late nineteenth century.

Detailed accounts of the Cheddar method date from an agricultural report of the late eighteenth century, but an exact recipe was not written down (or has not survived) for another 50 years. None the less, the routines associated with the cheese may have spread beyond the region earlier than this implies. Improvements in agriculture in the late nineteenth century benefited the cheese-makers, who made advances in both techniques and equipment, including the invention of the cheese mill and careful work on time, temperature and hygiene. Once perfected, the method became so identified with the cheese that it was known as 'cheddaring'. This was generously exported around the world by the British, who left a trail of upstart 'Cheddars' whenever they colonized an area deemed suitable for production.

The centralization of cheese-making during 1939–45 had significant effects on Cheddar. Firstly, official requirements for cheese to be of a specified moisture content (to enhance keeping qualities) led to the elimination of moister types. Secondly, the number of farms who resumed production after the war was greatly reduced. The introduction of rindless, block cheeses and frequent use of pasteurized milk further reduced the unique characteristics of Cheddar made in South Western England. Proliferation of *soi-disant* Cheddars blurred the popular concept of the real thing.

Farmhouse cheese-making survives in the area, although some of the operations are semi-industrial in scale. Some makers still use unpasteurized milk to make truckle cheeses. A recent development is the introduction of rennet of vegetable origin, to cope with the increased demand for vegetarian foods.

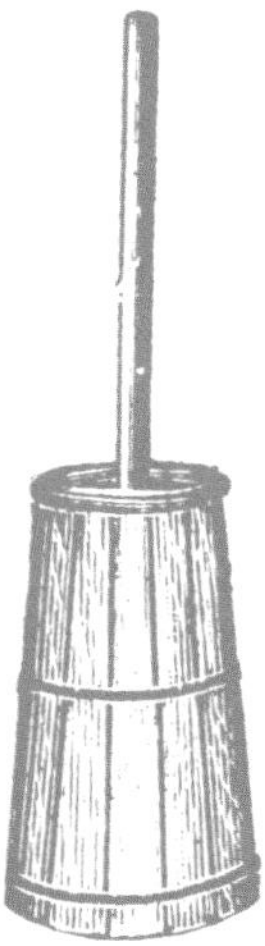

The designation Cheddar is unprotected, and much inferior cheese is made elsewhere under this name. 'West Country Farmhouse Cheddar Cheese' has been awarded Protected Designation of Origin (PDO).

TECHNIQUE:

Cheddar cheese is produced by many manufacturers, large and small, using the basic recipe with slight individual variations. Both pasteurized and unpasteurized milk are used, according to the maker's preference. The milk is heated to about 21°C and inoculated with starter culture (1–2 per cent, 5–15 minutes ripening); rennet is added and stirred in. After 30–40 minutes, cutting is begun, gently, to give curd pieces the size of wheat grains; once cut, stirring begins as the heat is raised. The curds and whey are thoroughly heated in the vat, and the temperature increased to 40°C over 40–50 minutes; the curd is continuously stirred until the correct firmness is achieved (judging this can only be achieved by experience). Acidity at this point is crucial; once the correct level is achieved, stirring ceases; the curd starts to mat, and the whey is run off. Cutting and turning, or cheddaring, is carried out either in the vat, or on a shallow tray or cooler. The object is to expel as much whey as possible. Firstly a centre portion of curd is removed to create a drainage channel; then the remainder is cut into large blocks which are turned; after 5–10 minutes the blocks are cut into smaller strips which are turned and piled higher; this process of cutting and turning continues for up to 90 minutes until the curd is judged sufficiently cool, well drained and acid. The curd is put through a curd mill to break it up. The curd is turned with a fork to keep it friable and allow salt to be mixed evenly (1kg salt to 45kg curd). The curd is broken into small pieces and put into cloth-lined moulds. The moulds are piled on top of each other to commence pressing, then placed in horizontal gang presses (in which several cheeses are pressed at once); when the whey starts to be expelled, the pressure is increased for 24–48 hours; the cheese is turned out 2–4 hours after the first pressing; the cloth wrung out in warm water and replaced and the cheese returned to the press; the next day the cheese is bathed for 5–10 seconds in warm water and returned to the press with light pressure; later the same day, the cheese is changed into a dry cloth and greased with melted lard which is rubbed thoroughly into the surface of the cheese; then the cheese is pressed for another 24 hours; after removal from the press, another bandage is applied. Ripening is at 8–9°C and a relative humidity of 86°; the cheeses are turned every day and cleaned to remove mould.

The production of block cheddar is similar until the moulding stage is reached. Then it is pressed into blocks. On removal from the press, it is wrapped in film to exclude air, and the cheeses are then strapped under pressure and transferred to the ripening room.

Cheddars sell at various degrees of maturity: mild (6 months after making); mature (9–12 months); extra-mature (over 12 months).

REGION OF PRODUCTION:

SOUTH WEST ENGLAND.

Clotted Cream and Clotted-Cream Butter

DESCRIPTION:

CLOTTED CREAM IS THICK, WITH A SOLID, PALE GOLDEN CRUST. IT CONTAINS 55–60 PER CENT BUTTERFAT.

HISTORY:

Clotting cream is really a means of lightly preserving it; when ordinary cream has been transformed into clotted cream it will keep in a cool place for about 2 weeks, as opposed to a few days. The method is probably very ancient and similar products are known in western Asia. Early references to clotted, or clouted, cream can be found in English texts from the sixteenth century onwards. The first mention cited by the *Oxford English Dictionary* is Boorde's *Dyetary of Helth* (1542). A multitude of descriptions and references exist from the seventeenth century and later. Even the earliest references make clear that it was a regional product. Recipes show that the method for making it has remained essentially unchanged for 400 years.

This is a region with a mild climate, rich pasture lands, and a traditional cattle breed yielding milk with a high butterfat content, all factors conducive to the development of specialist dairy produce. *Law's Grocer's Manual* (*c.* 1895) remarks on 'the increasing fancy for this delicacy'; that a regular sale for it was springing up in all large towns, and that the best was thought to come from Devon, notably the area around Ilfracombe. The cream was packed in small glazed pots for export to other parts of the country. Although the presumption is that clotted cream comes from Devon, it is equally known and long-established in Cornwall. The Devon connection probably took first place simply because it was the larger county, with wider connections to the country at large.

Once clotted, it was claimed the crust was sometimes solid enough to support a pound weight without breaking. Clotted cream has been used in the cookery of its region of origin (in breads, cakes, pastries, with fish, or as other regions might use cream); it is more generally thought of as a delicacy in its own right.

Clotting cream was also a very good way to turn milk into a flavourous butter. The heat-treatment required to make scalded cream and transforming the result into butter are 2 consecutive steps in preserving and adding value to a local raw material. 'This cream was stirred by hand, the maid putting her arm into the pot and stirring it until the butter came. In hot weather when the hand was too warm, a bottle was sometimes used' (Fussell, 1966). The existence of this butter was acknowledged by the author of the *General View of the Agriculture of the County of Devon* (1813) and, a century later, White (1932) writes about a Devonshire farmer's wife demonstrating making butter by beating clotted cream with her hand. There is a view current that this form of butter-making is now more known in Cornwall than Devon. Small amounts are still produced in the West Country for local consumption. No other region of Britain has developed clotted cream, or butter made from it, as a speciality. Awarded Protected Designation of Origin (PDO).

TECHNIQUE:

Clotted cream requires long slow heating at a moderate temperature. The craft method is as follows: both unpasteurized and pasteurized milk are used. Traditionalists prefer the excellent flavour of unpasteurized milk from Channel Island cattle which has a high butterfat content. The cream is separated from the milk and kept overnight; it may be ripened if desired. The cream, contained in enamel pans, is placed in a bain-marie and heated gently for about 2 hours. This process is crucial; the time and temperature must be correct; only experience will teach the right combination. The temperature of the bain-marie is maintained at below boiling, about 82°C. Once the correct golden, honeycomb crust has formed, the pans are removed from the heat. Industrial methods work on the same principle, but heating takes place either in an oven or in steam cabinets.

Before the advent of milk separators, cream would be clotted on the whole milk. First, the cream would be allowed to rise naturally on the pan of milk saved from one of the day's milk-ings. If the morning milk, it would be left until late in the afternoon; if the evening's, then left overnight. The pan was placed carefully over the fire and it was scalded, as described above. In small farmhouses, the pan would be placed over the kitchen hearth; in larger households, the dairy might have a special stove constructed from a stone slab pierced with holes big enough to accommodate the pans safely. A charcoal brazier could be placed beneath each pan. These pans were of brass or of earthenware. Once the cream was scalded and had clotted, it was skimmed off the milk and stored in flat dishes. Brears (1998) provides illustrations.

Clotted-cream butter is made on a small scale by craft producers. Instead of stirring the cream by hand, as was done in the past, an electric whisk is now used. The cream is whipped until crumbly and worked by hand to squeeze out as much moisture as possible. It is washed in cold water, then beaten with a boiled cloth on a wooden platter. It is pressed by hand into a mould to make round pats.

REGION OF PRODUCTION:

South West England, Devon and Cornwall.

Cornish Yarg Cheese

DESCRIPTION:

Pressed cow's milk cheese, with nettle leaves as a wrapping, made in 2 sizes, 15cm diameter and 25cm; both roughly 7cm high. Weight: 1kg and 3kg. Form: a truckle and a flat wheel. Colour: almost white curd, with a powdery grey rind that shows a pattern derived from the nettle leaves in which it is wrapped. Flavour and texture: a young Yarg cheese has a fresh, lemony flavour and a moist, crumbly curd; it softens as it matures, developing a deeper flavour.

HISTORY:

The use of leaves of common plants such as nettles as substrata for draining cheeses, or wrappings for the finished product, has a long history, though now unusual. 'Nettle Cheese' was mentioned in the seventeenth century by Gervase Markham, who considered that a new milk cheese ripened on nettles was 'the finest of all summer cheeses which can be eaten'.

Although Cornwall was never famous for cheese in the way of counties to the east, some was made. A recipe 'to make our good Cornish cheese' was published in *Farmhouse Fare*, a collection of recipes from farmers' wives all over the country. The details suggest that modern Cornish Yarg is not dissimilar. It was developed in the 1970s by Alan and Jennie Gray ('Yarg' is simply 'Gray' spelt backwards). It has been awarded a Protected Designation of Origin (PDO).

TECHNIQUE:

Milk from designated herds of local Friesian cattle is used; the milk is pasteurized. Starter is added, and the milk left for about an hour, before renneting with vegetarian rennet. It is then left for another hour. The curd is cut by hand, drained gradually and the mass stirred, recut and turned until considered dry enough. It is milled through a peg mill into pieces of about 50mm then filled into moulds. It is left under medium pressure for about 18 hours, after which it is unmoulded. Brining is for 6 hours. The cheeses are wrapped in nettle leaves; these encourage the growth of penicillium moulds essential for ripening. The cheeses are stacked in controlled humidity and temperature for 3 weeks, turned daily.

REGION OF PRODUCTION:

South West England, Cornwall.

Curworthy Cheese

DESCRIPTION:

Pressed, pasteurized and unpasteurized cow's milk cheese. There are 3 cheeses in this group, Curworthy, Devon Oke (the largest) and Belstone. Dimensions: 10cm diameter, 4.5cm deep (450g, Curworthy only); 12cm diameter, 5cm deep (1.1kg, Curworthy and Belstone); 15cm diameter, 6cm deep (2.3kg,

CURWORTHY AND BELSTONE); 16CM DIAMETER, 10CM DEEP (4.7KG, DEVON OKE). COLOUR: BUTTERY YELLOW, DARKER TOWARDS THE EDGES, WITH A FEW SMALL HOLES. TEXTURE AND FLAVOUR: SMOOTH, SWEET, WITH OVERTONES OF DRIED GRASS AND SHARP AFTERNOTE.

HISTORY:

The Curworthy recipe was devised in the early 1980s using old instructions for 'quick' cheeses from the South West combined with local expertise. Sources included Gervase Markham's *Country Contentments* (1620), Baxter's *Library of Agriculture* (1846) and Dorothy Hartley's recipe for slipcoat or slipcote (1954). Slipcoat is a term which was used quite widely in England until the beginning of the last century meaning either a cheese which burst its coat and was eaten young because it would never mature properly (usually referring to a Stilton), or a creamy, light-textured cheese to be eaten young, made with only a light, brief pressing – a category to which Curworthy belongs. The initial development was carried out by the *Farmer's Weekly* (the main trade journal for the farming community), Wanda and David Morton (farm managers working for the magazine) and the staff of the local Agricultural Development and Advisory Service. Curworthy is an emergent product; it began initially as an experiment in diversification. Having proved successful, the farm and recipe were acquired by the current makers in 1987 and output has increased steadily.

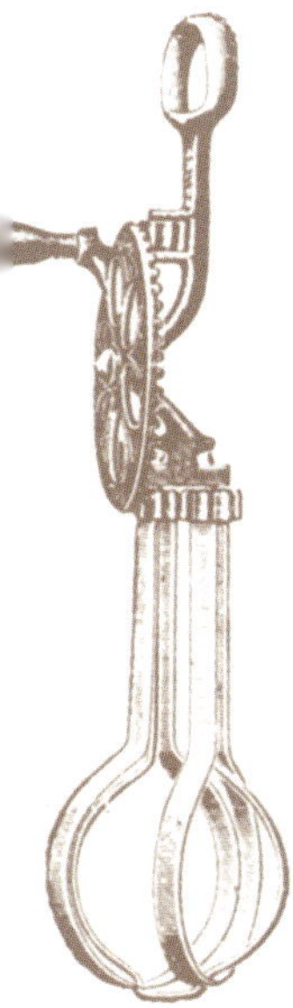

TECHNIQUE:

The same method is employed for all 3 cheeses. Animal rennet is used for Curworthy and Devon Oke, both of which can be of pasteurized or unpasteurized milk; Belstone is always made from unpasteurized, using vegetable rennet. Milk from a designated herd of Friesian cattle is used. The milk is pasteurized if required and then brought to the temperature necessary for cheese-making; starter and rennet are added. The curd is cut 2 ways, stirred and scalded to about 38°C, then drained and piled at one end of the vat, before being filled into the mould. It is pressed for about 2.5 hours, after which the cheese is removed and brined. Maturing varies with size, but is a minimum of 6 weeks for the smallest Curworthy and up to 6 months for Devon Oke.

REGION OF PRODUCTION:

SOUTH WEST ENGLAND, OKEHAMPTON (DEVON).

'Bachelor's fare: bread and cheese, and kisses.'

JONATHAN SWIFT

Dorset Blue Vinney Cheese

DESCRIPTION:

BLUE MOULD, HARD, SKIMMED COW'S MILK CHEESE, MADE IN CYLINDERS OF 1.35–2.3KG AND 6KG. COLOUR: CREAM OR YELLOW, WITH FINE BLUE-GREEN VEINS. FLAVOUR AND TEXTURE: STRONG, SHARP BLUE FLAVOUR; HARD TEXTURE.

HISTORY:

The word vinney derives from an archaic word vinew, which meant mould. It was in general use until the sixteenth century but was subsequently confined to South West dialect. Here, it was associated with a blue-mould cheese made in Dorset. This was certainly known in the eighteenth and nineteenth centuries as a cheese made by the wives of dairymen, using milk left after the cream had been removed for sale or conversion into butter. Thus it was always a very low-fat, rather hard cheese (Rance, 1982). Numerous recipes survive. The growth of blue mould in the cheese was regarded as the defining characteristic, and was encouraged by various methods, including placing the cheeses in barns or harness rooms to mature.

In the twentieth century, several factors adversely affected production: the secure market for whole, fresh milk provided by the Milk Marketing Board; the invention of efficient mechanical devices for separating milk and cream, which left no residual fat, producing a very hard cheese; and limits on cheese-makers imposed by the Ministry of Food during 1939–45. Until the 1970s, output remained low and the cheese was hard to find. A true Blue Vinney is once again available commercially.

TECHNIQUE:

The milk from morning milking is skimmed by hand. Skimmed-milk powder is added to adjust the fat content, to make a cheese suitable for modern taste. Starter culture, rennet from vegetable sources and penicillin mould are added. The curd is cut into 2cm cubes and left overnight. Next day, the curd is drained, cut into blocks, milled, salted and packed into moulds. These remain in a warm dairy for 5 days. The cheeses are unmoulded, spread with a paste of flour and blue mould, and ripened for 10 weeks to 5 months, with spiking after 1 month to encourage the spread of mould through the cheese. Dorset Blue has been awarded Protected Geographical Indication (PGI).

REGION OF PRODUCTION:

South West England, Dorset.

Double Gloucester Cheese

DESCRIPTION:

Hard, pressed, unpasteurized and pasteurized cow's milk cheese. Double Gloucester is made in a flat wheel about 30cm diameter, 12cm high, weighing about 11kg. Colour: pale orange to deep red-orange. Some cheeses have annatto added to the curd. Flavour and texture: mellow, round flavour and close creamy texture.

HISTORY:

Two cheeses are associated with Gloucestershire: Double Gloucester, and the less common, lower fat Single. Despite a common heritage, they are separate. The differences of method are subtle and the origin of the terms double and single obscure. They evolved in the late eighteenth century, when the traditional method for making 'best' cheese developed into one calling for the whole milk of 2 milkings, or the cream from an evening milking plus the whole milk from a morning milking (Rance, 1982). Double may refer to this use of 2 lots of milk. Alternatively, the terms may have meant nothing more than double being twice as thick as single (Black, 1989).

Gloucestershire, which includes both the Cotswolds and the low-lying land in the valley of the River Severn, has certainly produced cheese for a long time. Rance (1982) states that a regional cheese was exported in the eighth century AD. It is impossible to know what this was like. Fourteenth-century records show a Cotswold manor making cow's and sheep's milk cheeses and sending them to the nuns who owned the farm, in Caen in Normandy. If Gloucester cheese did incorporate sheep's milk, no trace of this habit has been found beyond this isolated record.

Evidence for cheese-making throughout the county during the early modern period can be seen in the tall farmhouses which contain a cheese-room on the third storey; domestic inventories also mention much cheese-making equipment. One area, the Vale of Berkeley, in the south, became very important. Possibly the local Gloucester breed of cattle, whose milk is particularly good for cheese-making, contributed to the excellence of their cheese.

At first, Gloucester was a coloured cheese made from the full-cream milk of a single milking. These were known as 'best' until Double Gloucester was recognized as a separate type at the end of the eighteenth century. The cheeses continued to have a high reputation, although disease reduced the population of Gloucester cattle and they were replaced by 'improved' breeds from the Midlands. Cheese production became factory-centred in the twentieth century. A little farmhouse cheese survived and renewed interest in old breeds led to the revival of Gloucester cattle and the use of their milk in cheese from the 1970s onwards.

Several folk customs are associated with cheeses in this region. One is the 'cheese rolling' on Whit Monday at Cooper's Hill, between Gloucester and Cheltenham. Four cheeses are rolled down the hill and chased by an assembled crowd. A similar merriment was recorded at Randwick.

TECHNIQUE:

Current practice is to make Double Gloucester from the whole milk of 2 milkings. It is heated to 28°C and starter is added. Annatto is mixed through the milk and then rennet is added and the milk left 45–60 minutes. The curd is cut into cubes of about 3mm and stirred for 20–40 minutes whilst the heat is raised to about 37°C. Stirring continues until the correct acidity is reached. The curd is allowed to settle and the whey drained off slowly. It is cut into fairly large blocks, piled and turned every 15 minutes as the acidity develops. Milling is through a fine curd mill; then salt is added (about 750g for each 45kg), stirred in thoroughly and allowed to dissolve. The curd is placed in moulds lined with cheese-cloth. Pressing continues for 2 days; the cheese is removed and turned once during this time, and increasing pressure is used on the second day. The cheese is ripened at 8°C and turned daily; then matured for 3–8 months.

REGION OF PRODUCTION:

WEST ENGLAND, GLOUCESTERSHIRE.

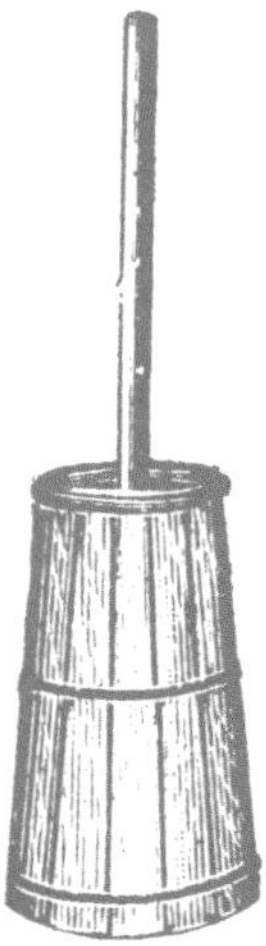

Single Gloucester Cheese

DESCRIPTION:

PRESSED, COW'S MILK CHEESE, ORIGINALLY MADE IN A WHEEL 6.5CM THICK, ABOUT 40CM DIAMETER, WEIGHING ABOUT 7KG. NOW MADE IN VARYING WEIGHTS, 900G–3.5KG. COLOUR: PALE LEMON. FLAVOUR: MILD, SWEET-SHARP, WITH CREAMY FINISH.

HISTORY:

Single Gloucester became distinct from the closely related Double Gloucester (see the entry above) at the end of the eighteenth century. Patrick Rance (1982) said that they were praised by William Marshall in 1796, who considered them equal to 'whole-milk cheeses from counties with poorer soil and less admirable cattle,' even though they were made partially from skimmed milk. Single Gloucester evolved as a lower-fat cheese, smaller in size. Unlike Double, it was not coloured. The making of Double Gloucester flourished in the Vale of Berkeley, whilst the Single was made on farms in the north and east of the county. They were more seasonal, some only made during the spring, and they were only matured for 2 months. They have never been as widely marketed as Double Gloucester and for much of the twentieth century only small amounts were made. Interest was renewed in the 1970s and it is now on sale again. Awarded Protected Designation of Origin.

TECHNIQUE:

This cheese uses a mixture of whole and skimmed milk. It is heated to 19°C and starter added, followed by a vegetarian rennet. The curd is left to set for about 1 hour and 40 minutes. The curd is cut, stirred to break it up further, and the heat is raised to 34°C. The curd is drained, cut into relatively small squares and turned. It is recut and turned at least twice more to make very small pieces. It is then sliced and milled through a Cheshire mill, and salt is added. It is filled into cheese-cloth-lined moulds. Pressing is for 48 hours, during which the cheese is removed, turned and put back in the cloth, then given a final pressing for 2 hours without the cloth. Maturing: 3–12 weeks.

REGION OF PRODUCTION:

West England, Gloucestershire, Devon.

Sharpham Cheese

DESCRIPTION:

Mould-ripened, soft, unpasteurized cow's milk cheese in 3 sizes. Weight: 250g; 500g; or 1kg. Form: the smallest cheese is square; the larger round. Colour: white mould crust with stripes from straw mat; deep rich yellow-cream. Flavour and texture: sharp and chalky when young, ripening to a soft creamy texture with mild mushroom flavour.

HISTORY:

Sharpham cheese belongs to the new cheeses which have arisen during the last 40 years as the artisan side of the industry began to revive from the damage inflicted by rationing during and after World War II. Several craftsmen have become well established in Devon, a county traditionally famous for dairy produce – in the early eighteenth century, the traveller Celia Fiennes noted that the dairy market in Exeter occupied 3 streets.

Experiments were carried on for some years at Sharpham House, near Totnes, before the present recipe was evolved. The particular type of milk used – from Jersey cattle – has a high butterfat content. Much background research was undertaken in France and, eventually, a Coulommiers type (widely taught in Britain and popular with small cheese-makers throughout the last century) proved successful. Sharpham has been sold since the early 1980s.

TECHNIQUE:

Milk from the Sharpham Estate Jersey herd is first flash-heated and cooled. Starter is added, and the milk ripened, vegetable rennet and a penicillin strain are added. The curd is cut by hand and separated from the whey; some of the whey is scooped off after a few minutes and the curd cut again; then it is hand-ladled into moulds and drained. The cheeses are turned, drained further and salted. Maturing is at a relatively warm temperature for about a week; then they are left for the mould to develop. They are wrapped and transferred to cooler temperatures to finish ripening.

REGION OF PRODUCTION:

South West England, Totnes (Devon).

Vulscombe Cheese

DESCRIPTION:

Soft goat's cheese, in rounds 6cm diameter, 4cm deep. Weight: about 180g. Colour: white. Flavour: creamy, dense, slight lemon tang, very mild goat flavour. Variants are flavoured with herbs and garlic, or with crushed black peppercorns.

HISTORY:

This is one of many goat's milk cheeses which have become so important in British artisan manufacture during the last 40 years. Before, with the exception of a few families who kept milking-goats as a hobby or to provide milk for children allergic to that of cows, not many paid attention to making goat's cheese and none reached the market place. During the 1960s and 1970s, interest in self-sufficiency and small-holding led to the greater popularity of goat's milk products. This was given extra momentum by changes in agriculture and the necessity for diversification in the 1980s. There are now many well-established makers of goat's cheese, spread throughout Britain, with concentrations in Kent and Sussex, North Yorkshire, Cumbria and the Scottish Borders. Though receiving little support from government and small in volume, this is a dynamic and creative sector. Recipes may be inspired by French examples or British originals evolved through trial and error. It is impossible to list them all. British taste generally leans towards young, cream-textured cheeses characterized by a mild goat flavour and slightly acid freshness, although some people do make mould-ripened, soft cheeses, or hard, pressed cheese, or blue cheeses using goat's milk. Vulscombe is based on the acid curd method, used by cottagers and farmers' wives during the eighteenth and nineteenth centuries to make small quantities of fresh soft cheese for immediate consumption.

TECHNIQUE:

British goat cheeses are a diverse subject and it is impossible to discuss them all. One which represents the general taste for mild creaminess has been selected. Vulscombe is named for the valley where it is made. The area has a mixed farming economy in which dairy products are important. The cheese derives from the milk of one herd of goats grazing old-established, flower-rich pastures at an altitude of about 250 metres in central Devon. Supplementary hay and silage are fed in winter and a grain-based concentrate is used for lactating animals. Cheese-making begins once 3 milkings have been accumulated. The temperature is raised to 10°C and a cultured starter added. Then it rises to 32°C over some hours and incubation continues until the milk has separated into curds and whey. Straining is through muslin and cheese-cloth for about 36 hours, then the curd is salted and herbs or peppercorns added if appropriate. It is ladled into moulds and pressed lightly for 24 hours.

REGION OF PRODUCTION:

SOUTH WEST ENGLAND, DEVON.

Whey Butter

DESCRIPTION:

BUTTER MADE FROM THE WHEY. IN COLOUR IT IS PALE GOLD; IN FLAVOUR, IT IS DESCRIBED AS 'NUTTY' OR SLIGHTLY CHEESY, THIS DEEPENS WITH AGE.

HISTORY:

Whey butter has probably been produced by cheese-makers in Britain for many centuries. Whey is the by-product of cheese-making, a thin liquid separated from the curd in the early stages. Depending on the type of cheese, the whey carries with it a small proportion of butter-fat and, in some areas, this is collected and churned into butter. Val Cheke (1959) states that, in the early medieval period, one of the duties of the dairy maid was to make whey butter and there are many references from later centuries relating to this practice. Maria Rundell (1807) gave details of how to manage cream for whey butter, a process which required the whey to stand a day and a night before it was skimmed, then boiled, poured into a pan of cold water and skimmed again 'as the cream rises' – this is not unlike making clotted cream. She remarks, 'Where new-milk cheese is made daily, whey-butter for common and present use may be made to advantage.' This statement still holds true today, and it is made in many cheese-making areas.

TECHNIQUE:

Ordinary butter produced in Britain is made from cream separated from fresh milk. In contrast to this, the butterfat used for whey butter goes through the initial processes of cheese-making. The exact details of these vary from region to region, but include the steps of adding starter and rennet, and allowing the milk to ripen and curdle with the temperature at about 32°C. Once the curd has set, it is cut and stirred while the temperature is increased by a few degrees. After a certain time, which varies according to the type of cheese being made, the whey is drained off. It is this part of the process which gives the distinctive flavour to the butter. The whey, which has a fat content of about 0.5–1 per cent, is then put through a mechanical separator (centrifuge), yielding up the fat in the form of cream which is then churned by conventional methods, lightly salted (about 1 per cent), and packed for sale.

REGION OF PRODUCTION:

South West England.

Elver

DESCRIPTION:

Young eels about 4cm long, slender and thread-like. Colour: transparent, pale amber. Flavour: mildly fishy.

HISTORY:

Eels were once a staple of fish-day diet. Medieval household accounts devote more entries to them than almost any other species of fish (Woolgar, 1992). Small wonder, therefore, that their fry should be esteemed as delicacies. The River Severn has long been noted for the vast numbers of elvers it attracts. Neufville Taylor (1965) mentions an elver net in a domestic inventory dated 1587 and Daniel Defoe (1724–6) remarked on elver-cakes sold at Bath and Bristol. White (1932) states elvers in large baskets were being cried through the streets of Gloucester even after the First World War. The fish products of the Severn estuary were important regional symbols, whether the salmon, the elvers or the lampreys – the Corporation of Gloucester sent a lamprey pie to the reigning monarch every year until 1836.

Elvers are caught from the Somerset Levels up the Severn as far north as Tewkesbury. Villages some way from the bank have memories of elver cookery. FitzGibbon (1972) records instructions for elver pie (made as a sort of pasty) from the village of Keynsham, half way between Bristol and Bath on the River Avon.

Elvers have remained a popular food in the region, but they are now very expensive, and much of the catch is exported, some going as stock for eel-farms (Green, 1993). Further-more, a study undertaken by Brian Knights to investigate the declining catch of elvers from the Severn in the 1980s concluded that oceanic cycles had affected numbers.

There are several local methods for cooking elvers, including flouring and deep frying; and frying in bacon fat then adding eggs to make a type of omelette. Alternatively, they are steamed to make a loaf. There are elver-eating contests in the villages on the lower reaches of the Severn on Easter Monday. During the season, between the spring tides of March and April, fresh elvers can be bought from local markets.

TECHNIQUE:

The elvers are caught at night by inhabitants who have rights to particular places on the river where swift-moving water comes close to the bank. They take up station some time before the 'bore', a high wave formed by the incoming tide in the Severn estuary as it narrows, and warn each other of its arrival by shouting a message along the river, marking its progress. As the tide begins to ebb, nets are put into the water with their mouth facing downstream to catch the elvers as they swim upstream against the flow; after a few minutes a net is removed and emptied, then dipped again. A suspended light can be used to attract the fish. If the run is poor, the net may be 'tealed', pegged in position for some time, in an attempt to maximize the catch.

REGION OF PRODUCTION:

WEST ENGLAND, SEVERN ESTUARY AND TRIBUTARIES.

Smoked Mackerel

DESCRIPTION:

Single fillets of smoked mackerel with skin. Colour: chestnut brown on flesh surface, cream internal flesh. Flavour: woody-oily, lightly salty.

HISTORY:

Similar to the herring, with a high oil content, mackerel flesh spoils rapidly when fresh and the hot-smoking process over oak chips was a method of processing which the curers have developed and which has become as popular as kippers. Mackerel is fished all around the British coasts, and has long been a mainstay of the South West. In the early twentieth century, the catch was preserved by canning (in Cornwall) or salting (in parts of Scotland). When the herring fishery declined in the 1970s, processors turned their attention to mackerel as an alternative. Particularly good catches were made off the Cornish coast and a substantial smoking industry developed, using both whole fish and fillets.

When the Scottish herring fisheries were closed in 1977 to conserve stocks, attitudes there (where mackerel had hitherto been regarded as inferior) changed and catches began to increase; smoking was also taken up as a means of using the catch.

TECHNIQUE:

Made with fish caught mostly during December–February when they have an oil content of about 23 per cent. They are filleted to remove head and bone. Single fillets with the skin on are cured in a brine, placed on stainless-steel trays and cold-smoked for an hour then hot-smoked for 2 hours. Flavourings (pepper, herbs and spices) are sprinkled over before they are smoked.

REGION OF PRODUCTION:

South West England; also Scotland; East Anglia.

Bath Chaps

DESCRIPTION:

WEIGHT: 400–600G, DEPENDING ON THE AGE AND BREED OF PIG. COLOUR: BATH CHAP HAS THE APPEARANCE OF A CONE CUT IN HALF VERTICALLY; THE CURVED UPPER SURFACE IS COVERED WITH LIGHT BROWN OR ORANGE BREAD CRUMBS; WHEN CUT, THE CHAP IS STREAKED IN LAYERS OF PINK LEAN AND WHITE FAT. FLAVOUR: SIMILAR TO ENGLISH COOKED HAMS OF THE YORK TYPE.

HISTORY:

A Bath chap is the cheek of a pig, boned, brined and cooked. Why this delicacy should be associated with the town of Bath is not clear, except that it lies in an area which has been a centre of bacon curing.

Pig's cheeks have probably been cured and dried for as long as any other part of the animal. The word chap is simply a variant on chop which, in the sixteenth century, meant the jaws and cheeks of an animal. These are probably what Mrs Raffald (1769) intended when she gave a recipe 'To salt chops' with salt, saltpetre, bay salt and brown sugar. This called for the meat to be dried afterwards; it would be expected to keep for several months. A century later, Mrs Beeton gave a method for drying and smoking pig's cheeks, observing that 'A pig's cheek, or Bath chap, will take about 2 hours after the water boils.' *Law's Grocer's Manual* (*c.* 1895) notes both upper and lower jaws were used, the lower, which was meatier and contained the tongue, selling at about twice the price of the upper. Several manufacturers are recorded, including Hilliers of Stroud and the Wiltshire Bacon Company (founded at the end of the nineteenth century). However, today, only 2 producers have been located.

Bath chaps are eaten at main meals, usually with mustard. They are sold already cooked.

TECHNIQUE:

Bath chaps are no longer dried, merely lightly brined. They are cut from the pig's heads, cleaned, and boned. They are brined for a short time, after which they are cooked. Subsequently, they are pressed in a

I am passionate about the use of local food and the high quality of produce to be found in Devon is one of the main reasons I chose to move here to start my latest venture. I have spent a lot of my time driving around the county, sourcing suppliers, going to farmers markets, visiting smallholders, speaking to day-boat fishermen and building up a network of people who are as passionate and mad about food as we are here at the New Angel. I love anticipating what produce is going to be brought into the restaurant on any given day. Take asparagus for example: because the season only lasts for six weeks, there is always an air of anticipation around their delivery. Devon asparagus is excellent and dishes containing my favourite vegetable always fly out of the door. Likewise, it's great when Anthony Buscombe and his brother come straight in from their boat to the restaurant with a big box of freshly caught crab – 80 per cent of all of Britain's crab comes from the Dartmouth and Salcombe coast, and it's the best there is. The delicate, sweet meat needs only a little butter and spice, and I'm very lucky to be able to source such quality from my own doorstep. I regard this county as a centre of excellence for locally produced food. No other area can match Devon's variety of produce, and that is why I believe it is so important to promote and support local food producers, suppliers and small farming businesses.

John Burton Race

CHEF AND PROPRIETOR, THE NEW ANGEL, DARTMOUTH

mould to give the cone shape; when cold and set, the chaps are removed from their moulds and dusted with crumbs.

REGION OF PRODUCTION:

WILTSHIRE AND SOMERSET; SOUTH ENGLAND

Bradenham Ham (Fortnum Black Ham)

DESCRIPTION:

AN UNSMOKED CURED HAM FOR COOKING. WEIGHT: ABOUT 14KG. COLOUR: THE SKIN IS BLACK, THE FAT BROWN-TINTED. FLAVOUR: DELICATE, SWEET, MILD.

HISTORY:

The Bradenham Ham Company of Wiltshire produced hams according to a recipe dated 1781 (Simon, 1960). The recipe is thought to be named for the last Lord Bradenham. It emanated from Bradenham in Buckinghamshire. The secret is in the immersion in molasses and spices, resulting in a sweet-tasting meat. Recipes for treacle-cured hams appeared in domestic cookery books at this time, and the developing West India trade provided molasses a-plenty. The hams were hung and matured for a longer period than other, less exclusive products. In the novel *A Rebours* (1884), the decadent hero visits an English restaurant in Paris, passing at the entrance a counter displaying 'hams the mellow brown of old violins'.

The curing method and the trademark of a flying horse were the exclusive property of the Bradenham Ham Co. which was awarded a Royal Warrant in 1888. In 1897 the Wiltshire Bacon Company took over Bradenham Ham but continued to produce at Chippenham in Wiltshire. When that company closed in its turn, production was moved to Yorkshire. Similar recipes are used by other curers; Brunham, made in Wiltshire, is one example.

TECHNIQUE:

The legs, cut from bacon pigs, must carry a specified level of fat otherwise they become dry; they are long-cut, giving a rounded shape.

Curing begins in dry salt with saltpetre and sugar but, after an unspecified time, the hams are removed and placed in a marinade of molasses and spices, after which they are hung to mature. The process from fresh meat to fully matured ham takes 5–6 months.

REGION OF PRODUCTION:

South West England, Wiltshire.

Brawn

DESCRIPTION:

Small pieces of brined pork, usually from the head and shoulder, set in a jelly. In appearance, it is a translucent, pale gold-brown with pieces of pale meat and sometimes chopped herbs; the meat is brined and finely shredded for some versions, giving an opaque, pink appearance; in the North-East, brawn is coloured a bright orange-red. Brawn should be highly flavoured; sage and black pepper are favourite seasonings.

HISTORY:

One element of the history of brawn is constant right down to the present day and this is not the composition of the dish itself but the habit of serving it with mustard. 'Furst set forth the mustard and brawne of boore ye wild swyne,' instructed the *Boke of Nurture* in 1460.

> 'Good bread and good drinke,
> a good fier in the hall,
> brawne, pudding and souse,
> and good mustard withall'

was Thomas Tusser's (1573) prescription for a husbandman's Christmas. Later recipes for brawn sauce made of mustard, sugar and vinegar abound (e.g. Dallas, 1877).

Brawn originally meant muscle or meat of any description; by the fifteenth century the word was particularly, although not exclusively, associated with the flesh of wild boar. The Tudor physician Thomas Cogan stated that the flesh of wild swine was better for you than any tame animal and that brawn, which is the flesh 'of a boare long fedde in the stie,' was difficult of digestion. He counselled that it should be eaten at the start of a meal – advice that seems to have been followed, even if unconsciously, unto the present day (O'Hara May, 1977). Because the word applied exclusively to flesh or muscle meat, it followed that brawn developed the restricted meaning of the boned flesh, fat and skin, as opposed to the whole joint, bone-in. The way such a floppy joint was best dealt with was that it would be collared. It would be rolled up tight, wrapped in cloth and tied round [collared] with tape or string before boiling. Collaring was normally done to sides of pig, rather than hams. In the sixteenth-century accounts of the Star Chamber brawn appears almost monotonously as collars or rounds. Martha Bradley (1756) has instructions on choosing brawn. Her definition of the word was meat that came from an uncastrated boar (not necessarily wild). The best was from a young animal: old boar was too tough and the rind too thick, meat from a sow too soft. Her namesake, Richard Bradley, writing 20 years earlier (1736), disagreed. His brawn was the collared flitches of 'an old boar, for the older he is, the more horny will the brawn be'. He thought brawn rather insipid; horny was probably a good thing.

A collar was a convenient package that could be cooked and sliced. The method was also a way of preserving unwieldy and quick-spoiling food, in other words, pickling. Collared meats (and fish) were usually brined and spiced, boiled, pressed and sliced. Brawn came to mean almost exclusively pork cooked in this manner. If the meat was pressed and cooled in its liquor, it would indeed begin to look like the jellied brawn we have today.

Whereas at the outset brawn applied to most parts of the pig apart from the valuable hams, by the 1800s, in the southern part of England, it had come to mean a dish based on pigs' heads, collared.

This appears under the title 'Tonbridge Brawn' in Eliza Acton (1845). As the head was the boniest (and least vendible) part of the animal, it was a natural candidate for collaring and repackaging, leaving the rest for bacon, ham or roasting joints. A dish that was also common in Georgian recipe books was 'mock brawn': a flank of pork rolled around morsels from calves' feet and pig's head, cooked, pressed and cooled. Gradually, as brawn was relegated to a dish of the poor and country people who killed their own pigs, the dish was simplified into a highly seasoned, moulded, meat jelly containing small pieces of pork.

Pork cheese, once commonly termed head cheese, is a similar dish made from finely minced meat rather than chopped scraps. In some regions, especially the North, brawn-type dishes are made from beef.

Brawn is still widely made, and is a profitable by-product of pork butchery. It is a component of salad lunches and still eaten with mustard or strong condiments. Although it may be found in many parts of the country, it is most often sold in the South West, where a number of relics of a once important industry survive, such as Bath chaps, chitterlings and the like.

TECHNIQUE:

The meat for brawn, usually pigs' heads, is cleaned thoroughly and brined for a few hours. It is boiled with seasonings, bones and feet until very well cooked. The mixture is strained, the meat picked off the bones and placed in moulds, the stock reduced and poured over, and the whole allowed to set. Where a colour is given to the brawn, suppliers would once have offered 'Indian Red' colouring agent.

REGION OF PRODUCTION:

SOUTH WEST ENGLAND.

Cornish Pasty

DESCRIPTION:

A baked pasty with many different fillings which are invariably raw when the pasty is made up. The shape is a pointed oval, with a seam of crimped pastry running the length of the pasty about one-third of the way in from the edge. Individual versions vary in their forms; industrially produced ones are more likely to be semi-circular. A mean size might be 20cm long, 10cm wide, and 4cm deep, weighing 330g. Colour: golden pastry (egg-washed). Flavour: beef and potato predominate.

HISTORY:

'A bit of pastry is everything to a Cornish household. I can remember the sense of shock when I visited my up-country in-laws for the first time and neither they nor their five daughters had a rolling pin' (Merrick, 1990).

Pasty is an old English word for a pie of venison or other meat baked without a dish (*OED*). Samuel Pepys consumed great numbers of them, as his diary relates. However, the use of the word declined in a large part of England and the only region where it survives is that stronghold of pastry, the South West, especially Cornwall. Here, the form settled into a fixed type: a pie that was food for the working man and his family. Spicer (1948), collecting regional recipes in the 1940s, remarked that pasties were originally baked on an iron plate set on the hearth, covered with an iron bowl, with ashes and embers heaped around. The Cornish were part of the English highland tradition which used a bakestone and pot-oven rather than the masonry or brick oven of champion country. Under the dialect name fuggan, references to pasties can be traced back to the mid-nineteenth century (Wright, 1896–1905), defined as 'an old Cornish dish… which is a pasty of very thick crust filled with potatoes'.

Tradition states that such food was the portable midday meal of miners and farm labourers, and that the Cornish will put anything in a pasty – meat, fish, bacon, cheese, vegetables, eggs or, in times of dearth, wild herbs. Potatoes, onions, leeks and turnips are allowed, but carrots are not customary; nor is minced, as opposed to chopped, meat. Fishermen, ideal beneficiaries of the convenience of the pasty, in fact eschew it. It is thought bad luck to bring one on a boat (Merrick, 1990). Pasties were often made too large to consume at a single sitting, and their ingredients were varied according to individual preference. Cooks would therefore mark each pasty with the initials of each intended recipient so that they could take up the relic they left off, and avoid a nasty surprise at the first bite.

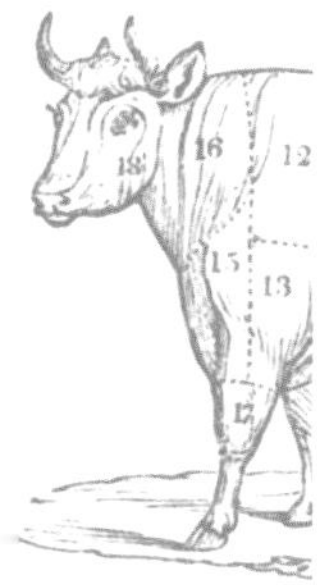

The pasty's success has been contagious since World War II. There are manufacturers everywhere. This may lead to variations, for example Priddy Oggie, sometimes quoted as a long-standing regional dish, is a pork-filled pasty with a cheese pastry which was invented in the late 1960s in Somerset.

TECHNIQUE:

A shortcrust pastry is usual, although some makers prefer something very like puff. This is rolled and cut to a circle 20cm across. A mixture of roughly equal quantities of raw, chopped beef steak and thinly sliced, raw potato, plus half as much chopped onion and turnip is well seasoned with salt and pepper. The filling is placed on one side of the pastry, the edge brushed with egg and excess pastry folded over to enclose it. The edge is crimped to seal, the outside egg-washed. It is baked at 200°C for 20 minutes, then 180°C for 40 more.

REGION OF PRODUCTION:

South West England.

Devon Cattle

DESCRIPTION:

Dressed carcass weight for steers aged 500 days is 190–300kg; for heifers, 160–300kg. The Devon is a fairly long animal. The flesh is finely grained, well-marbled and tender, with an excellent flavour.

HISTORY:

These cattle, which gain two alternative names, Red Devon or Ruby Red, from their dark, red-brown pelts, are traditional to Exmoor – hence a third, North Devons. Even in the Domesday Book (1086), the density of cattle recorded in north-west Devon was exceptional. This may hint, perhaps, at the emergence of a distinctive breed, although the first known mention of red cattle in the West Country was in correspondence of the late sixteenth century. In the eighteenth century, detailed descriptions of Devon cattle were given by several agriculturists. By this time the breed was improved to produce a stronger animal for heavy draught work. The foundations for these changes were laid by the Quartly family, who had acquired a farm on Exmoor. Comment thereafter stresses both the docility of the cattle and the quality of the beef. The Breed Society was formed in the late nineteenth century.

There is another Devon breed, the South Devon, which is recognized as distinct; it is a dual-purpose cow which provides excellent rich milk and good beef. Although coming from the same original strain, it is a heavier beast than the Ruby Red. It is touched upon in the entry for Channel Island milk.

TECHNIQUE:

The Red Devon cattle of Exmoor, where the breed was developed, are on the small side; this is because they were expected to fatten on sparse moorland pasture which is susceptibleto trampling into mud (the rainfall is very high) and responds well to the lightness of the Red Devons' feet. Exmoor is now an Environmentally Sensitive Area. Breeders on the lower, lusher pastures of Somerset selected for larger cattle.

Recently, new blood from the French Saler breed (known sometimes as French Devons) has been used to improve conformation, particularly the quantity of fat carried on the brisket and at the top of the tail. The two strains have been interbred in the past, the Devon contributing genes to the Salers in the 1800s.

Animals destined for beef are slaughtered from the age of 18 months. Some butchers prefer an older animal, of about 3 years. Older cattle were favoured for beef production in Britain in the past, but in previous centuries they worked as draught animals for some years prior to slaughter. At present, the returns for keeping cattle at pasture longer than absolutely necessary are low. Devons are cross-bred with various dairy cattle including Friesians, whose offspring are known as black steers or heifers.

REGION OF PRODUCTION:

South West England, Devon.

Devonshire Ham

DESCRIPTION:

A smoked or unsmoked cured ham for cooking. Weight: 3.5–5.5kg. Form: hams made in Devon were long-cut; the current maker trims the broad ends of the hams following a natural curve in the meat, and removes the skin, except at the knuckle end where it is cut into a zig-zag pattern in a style known as Florentine. Colour: white fat, deep rose lean. Flavour: a succulent texture and clean, pure ham flavour, with a light, fragrant oak smoke.

HISTORY:

Devonshire hams have been known for well over 150 years, and there is evidence that a particular ham cure existed in the area for a century before that. White (1932) quotes a Devon recipe for salting hams from the 1700s. Mrs Beeton (1861) gives a recipe for bacon or hams the Devonshire way, which shows the cure to have begun with dry-salting for 2 days, followed by brining in a pickle based on salt and sugar in proportions roughly 2:1. The hams were smoked for keeping and the pickle boiled and fortified with more salt and some black treacle before re-use. Anne Petch, the most prominent maker of hams currently working in this area, remarks that sugar or treacle in the cure helped to act as preservative and flavouring before saltpetre was available in a reliable form; it also counteracted the effects on flavour and texture which large quantities of salt had on the ham. *Law's Grocer's Manual* (*c.* 1895) mentions that 'Devonshire long cut hams – smoked or pale dried, and produced in the district round Plymouth – are also highly popular.' By the 1930s, the Devonshire cure, whilst remaining a brine cure, had lost much of its sweetness. A recipe collected from a farmer's wife between the world wars requires only a little treacle added to a salt and water brine.

TECHNIQUE:

Devonshire's rural economy places emphasis on dairy products, apple orchards, and pig-rearing. The climate is damp and mild and, consequently, the local ham cure is brine-based. The hams now made in Devon are by a producer who uses English breeds of pig, and oversees the entire process from raising the animal to marketing. The animals are farmedextensively, on open pasture, finished with a mixed grain feed of barley and wheat, andslaughtered at 6–7 months. After cutting from the carcass, the hams are trimmed, then brined for 12 days in a 60 per cent brine. They are smoked, if required, in cold smoke from oak, plus a little beech. The hams are aged for 3–4 weeks. They may be dispatched raw, boiled plain, or cooked with cider and spices, a local method.

REGION OF PRODUCTION:

SOUTH WEST ENGLAND, DEVON.

Dorset Horn Sheep

DESCRIPTION:

DRESSED CARCASS WEIGHT ABOUT 18–19KG.

HISTORY:

The Dorset Horn is indeed a Dorset sheep. This sparsely populated area, dominated by rolling chalk hills, has a long connection with the beast. The breed may have evolved from the now-rare Portland, a relic of the old tan-faced primitives once widely known in Britain and centred in the South West (Hall & Clutton-Brock, 1989). Further details are mysterious, although the influence of Merino blood is postulated. For a long time, the Dorset has been favoured for its extended breeding season. This was exploited to provide out-of-season lamb. In the mid-1700s, a manual of husbandry described the production of 'Dorset House Lambs' in Essex during late autumn for the London Christmas market. Such meat was associated with status; William Kitchiner (1817) remarked, 'House lamb is ... prized merely because it is unseasonable and expensive,' and Mrs Beeton (1861) commented on the system of intensive rearing pursued 'to please the appetite of luxury'. A flock book was established in 1892 and the breed has continued to bevalued. The intensive rearing system was abandoned before the First World War, but the Dorset Horn and the relatively new Polled Dorset are still used to provide young, new-season's lamb.

TECHNIQUE:

Lambing time can be adjusted to the demands of the market. The ewes breed from a young age and are excellent milkers. On mixed farms where lamb is just one part of the business, farmers tend to concentrate on producing meat for Christmas and New Year and then through to Easter. The lambs are born between mid-September and November; the flocks may be housed at lambing for ease of management and protection from predators. Shelter is otherwise unnecessary. Soon after lambing, the flocks are turned out to graze on the flush of autumn grass which follows hay- and silage-making. Sheep farmers who keep Dorset Horns produce 3 crops of lambs every 2 years.

REGION OF PRODUCTION:

SOUTH WEST ENGLAND.

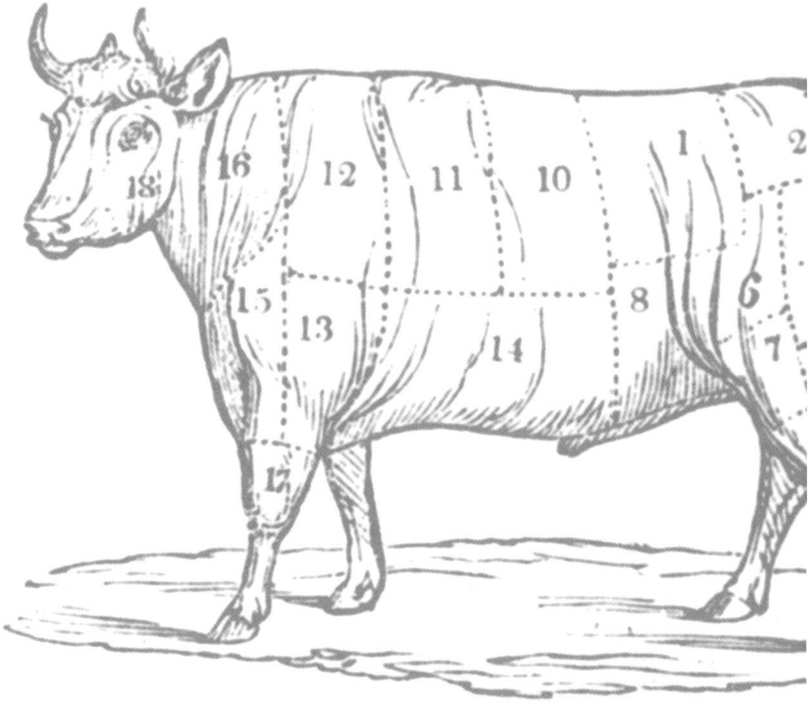

'Methinks sometimes I have no more wit than a Christian or an ordinary man has; but I am a great eater of beef, and I believe that does harm to my wit.'

WILLIAM SHAKESPEARE, *TWELFTH NIGHT*

Gloucestershire Old Spots Pig

DESCRIPTION:

Usually slaughtered to yield a porker of 50–55kg after dressing; it is a dual-purpose animal which can, if desired, be grown to reach bacon weight. It is characterized by large, irregular black spots on the skin which leave marks after the bristles have been removed; otherwise, the meat is deep pink, well-marbled, with white fat and a pale skin. Flesh is tender, succulent, with an excellent flavour. Here is pig which makes excellent crackling.

HISTORY:

The breed developed in response to farming conditions of the 1800s which required a hardy animal that could flourish on a varied diet. The Severn Valley in which the race evolved is a cheese and cider region and excess whey and windfall apples formed part of its diet, as well as household and garden waste. It is sometimes referred to as an orchard pig, because of where it prospered. Gloucestershire Old Spots were first noted in the early twentieth century, when the Breed Society was formed. It was then talked of as an ancient breed and the word 'Old' has always been part of the name, implying a long history. A Gloucester pig was noted in the 1850s but was described as white with large wattles. It is possible the breed arose from these Gloucesters crossed with Saddle-backs or unimproved Berkshires, black animals whose genes may have contributed the spots.

A drive towards home production of bacon by the British government in the 1930s led to a decline in numbers of Old Spots. It is slower maturing than improved animals and the spots were disliked. A trend towards leaner meat also worked against its use for pork. Breeders have eliminated all but a token spot. In the 1970s, renewed interest in rare breeds led to conservation of breeding stocks and reintroduction of old strains to modern farming and the food chain. This has been quite successful with Gloucestershire Old Spots.

TECHNIQUE:

The breed has a strong following in the Severn valley and environs. It is popular with hobby farmers who keep a few animals. The blotched skin is currently thought less of a problem and the spots have been bred back in. The pigs now resemble those known earlier last century. It is still used to forage apple and pear orchards by some farmers; whey, generated by West-Country cheese-making, is also available. These are supplemented with grain-based rations; the pigs may also be turned out to feed on residues of arable crops or on specially grown forage crops. It is still renowned as hardy, requiring minimal accommodation. The sows are good mothers. The breed is slow to mature, reaching a weight for slaughter as pork at 18–22 weeks.

REGION OF PRODUCTION:

SOUTH WEST ENGLAND.

Gloucester Sausage

DESCRIPTION:

UNCOOKED, FRESH PORK SAUSAGE, WEIGHING 75–100G – LARGER THAN OTHER FRESH SAUSAGES; PALE PINK; SHORT LINKS; GOOD, RICH FLAVOUR, WITH HERBS.

HISTORY:

Many Gloucester butchers include 'Gloster sausages' in their display. No early references have been located, but oral tradition is that they have been made for as long as anyone can remember. One factor in their excellence is the distinctive pig, Gloucestershire Old Spots. This produces fine fresh pork, hence also sausages. In a letter dated 1766, the Georgian man of fashion, Gilly Williams, wrote to his friend George Selwyn anticipating a meeting near the city. 'We shall eat Gloucester chine together,' he mused. Here, at least, there is a conjunction of Gloucester and pork that goes back a while.

TECHNIQUE:

Gloucestershire Old Spots are raised extensively on grain, dairy by-products and windfall apples, resulting in succulent, well-flavoured meat with good marbling, excellent for sausage making. The Gloucester recipe is not exceptional, using minced lean and fat pork, plus cereal (in the form of rusk) and a seasoning of herbs, salt and pepper. They are filled into natural casings.

REGION OF PRODUCTION:

West England, Gloucester.

Hog's Pudding

DESCRIPTION:

A cooked pork and cereal sausage; about 3 cm diameter and of varying lengths. Colour: a greyish-white or mottled pink and white; in some types the cereal can be seen as whole grains. Flavour: a bland combination of pork and cereal, overlaid by the spices favoured by the maker; some contain dried fruit.

HISTORY:

The first specific reference to hog's pudding in the *Oxford English Dictionary* is from the early eighteenth century. However, the word hog (used in English to mean a bacon pig since at least the fourteenth century), combined with recipes including spices and currants in a savoury dish, suggests the tradition is far older, with roots in medieval practice. White puddings of cereal, spices and dried fruit were known in the 1500s, and were probably made throughout southern England. Much later, Flora Thompson (1939) describes how the country dwellers of Oxfordshire used the various parts of a pig when it was killed in the winter months – hog's puddings bulked large.

Recipes varied; often they would have formerly included lights and spleen. Others emphasize the cereal content: a quotation from Hampshire (Wright, 1896–1905) describes it as 'the entrail of a pig stuffed with pudding composed of flour, currants and spice'. A late Victorian recipe from Sussex describes hog's puddings as small ball-like sausages, stuffed with pork, flour, spices and currants (White,

1932). Modern puddings have evolved from these heavily cereal-based, sweetish products. Although some containing fruit are still made, other examples are closer to a sausage, with groats (hulled, crushed cereal grains), lean pork and savoury spices, especially black pepper. In the past, they were used for any meal but now tend to be served at breakfast. The customary method of reheating was in simmering water, but they can be baked, fried or grilled.

TECHNIQUE:

Groats are soaked and cooked until soft, then mixed with minced pork, dried fruit and seasonings. This is filled into wide casings and tied in rings which are blanched in simmering water, just enough to cook the sausage through.

REGION OF PRODUCTION:

South England, especially South West.

Mendip Wallfish

DESCRIPTION:

'Wallfish' is a Somerset name for snails. The garden snail is the commonest variety; it has a brownish-ochre shell, about 3.5cm diameter.

HISTORY:

The use of snails as food is generally regarded by the British as curious and outlandish –more specifically, French. Evidence for their consumption in the past is patchy. Recipes used snails medicinally, to ease chest ailments. They are often found in early books of household remedies. A handful of culinary recipes were given by John Nott (1726). Roy Groves, who developed methods for the indoor farming of snails during the 1980s, states there is some oral evidence for snail eating in areas such as the North-East of England, where glass-blowing was an occupation. Snails reputedly have a beneficial effect on the respiratory system. Oral tradition also states that 'wallfish' are part of the diet in the West Country, particularly in the area around the

Mendips. Here, for about 50 years, the Miner's Arms (a pub and restaurant) at Priddy, has served snails as a house speciality.

Both the Roman snail (*Helix pomatia*) and the smaller garden snail (*Helix aspersa*) are found wild in Britain. *Law's Grocer's Manual* (*c.* 1895) remarked that both species were collected in England for the Paris market. Recent initiatives in agricultural diversification have also led to the foundation of a snail-farming industry with several producers of *Helix aspersa* in the Somerset area. Another species which is farmed is the African land snail.

TECHNIQUE:

Snails are collected from the wild in Somerset, but rarely reach the market, being consumed at home or sold to restaurants. The snails are collected in the autumn, and a proportion are frozen for use throughout the winter at the Miner's Arms. Snail farming is carried out at several locations, including at least one where the snails are reared outdoors in poly-tunnels. These enclose forage crops such as stubble turnips, to provide cover and help retain moisture. The snails take approximately a year to become fully grown. During winter they hibernate, when they are kept in boxes in barns, safe from predators. They are collected as required and sold alive.

REGION OF PRODUCTION:

SOUTH WEST ENGLAND, SOMERSET.

Wiltshire Bacon

DESCRIPTION:

SMOKED OR UNSMOKED CURED PORK FOR COOKING; A SIDE WEIGHS 29–31KG; THIS REPRESENTS HALF A PIG, TRIMMED AND CURED. COLOUR: DEEP ROSE-PINK LEAN, WHITE FAT. FLAVOUR: A MILD CURE.

HISTORY:

A reference dated 1794 which mentions the 'old' Wiltshire bacon, implies the area had been long known for this product (*OED*). The trade was based on both pigs native to the region and imported ones from Ireland which were driven across the county on their way to London markets. Mrs Beeton (1861) states the Wiltshire cure used dry salt and coarse sugar, the flitches lying in the pickle for a month before being hung to dry. One of the largest bacon curing companies in Britain, Harris of Calne, was started by a local butcher who took advantage of the herds of pigs passing his doorstep. In the mid-nineteenth century, the company began to use ice to chill the premises in the summer, an innovation allowing production the year round and the amount of salt in the cure to be reduced, making for sweeter, milder bacon. About this time a switch from dry to brine curing took place, to give the modern form of the cure, now practised in many areas outside its place of origin.

The bacon was sold after drying (when it was called green bacon in the South, and pale dried bacon in the north of England). If smoking took place, it was carried out by the wholesaler or retailer to suit their market. The south of the country showed a preference for smoked bacon. Large quantities of bacon are now imported into Britain. Until their Calne factory closed, Harris still produced Wiltshire bacon in its home region, but now there are only 2 commercial curers left in the area.

It should be noted that some bacon experts, for instance William Hogan (1978), use the term Wiltshire to refer to a cut as well as the cure. In this case it indicates half a pig, with the ham left on and the ribs intact but the blade bone removed.

TECHNIQUE:

A local manufacturer uses pigs reared on his own farm, fed on home-grown wheat and whey from the cheese industry in neighbouring Somerset. After cutting, the sides are immersed in a salt, saltpetre and water brine for 4–5 days. They are then stacked and drained for 14 days. The bacon may be smoked over hardwood sawdust. It is dispatched whole, in smaller joints, or sliced into rashers.

REGION OF PRODUCTION:

SOUTH WEST ENGLAND, WILTSHIRE.

Apple Cake

DESCRIPTION:

APPLE CAKE, SOMETIMES CALLED APPLE PUDDING, AND OFTEN GIVEN A COUNTY PREFIX DEPENDING ON THE PLACE OF ITS MAKING, IS USUALLY OBLONG OR SQUARE, BAKED IN A TRAY. ITS FLAVOUR PLAYS ON SWEET–ACID BALANCE, WHICH DEPENDS ON VARIETY OF APPLE USED: COOKING APPLES GIVE A MOISTER CAKE WITH AN ACID NOTE, DESSERT APPLES SWEETER AND MORE AROMATIC.

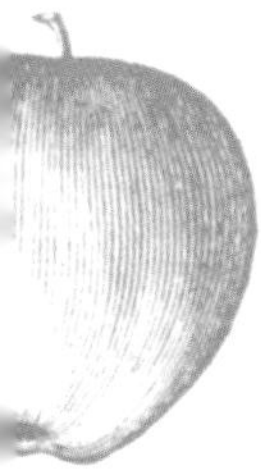

HISTORY:

Several modern recipes are found. They vary in concept; one from Cornwall is similar to a French *tarte Tatin*; one from Cambridgeshire appears related to German *Streusel*. However, a distinctively English version does exist in the South West, especially Dorset, Devon and Somerset. Here, raw apples are added to a plain cake at the outset, as if they were raisins or currants in a fruit cake. Apples have always been added to various cakes and puddings in apple country, but little documentary evidence survives. An example is a farmhouse recipe from Somerset (Webb, *c.* 1930). One from Dorset, 'one of the most famous of all English tea cakes', is in Spicer (1949). A modern collection asserts that Dorset apple cake is distinguished from others by being baked in separate tins before being sandwiched with butter (Raffael, 1997).

While popular in domestic circles and often made for sale in cafés, it can also be found in many craft bakeries in the region.

TECHNIQUE:

Apple cakes from the South West have minor variations in detail, such as addition of dried fruit and candied peel in a recipe from Dorset. They call for apples, flour, butter and caster sugar in the proportions 4:2:1:1. Chemical leavening is used. The apples (sour cooking apples are generally required, although some prefer eating apples because they are drier) are peeled, cored and sliced into segments. The butter is rubbed into the flour until the mixture resembles fine breadcrumbs. The sugar is stirred in, followed by sliced raw apple, and dried fruit and spices if required; the mixture is bound with egg and milk. It is scaled off into greased tins. The surface is levelled and sprinkled with granulated sugar. Baking takes 1 hour at 180°C.

REGION OF PRODUCTION:

South West England.

Bath Bun

DESCRIPTION:

A circular bun with nib sugar on the top and a highly glazed surface; diameter 60–70mm, depth 50mm. Weight: about 75g. Colour: golden brown with shiny glaze, sprinkled with currants and sugar. Flavour and texture: lightly spiced and sweetened, close textured, with lump sugar underneath.

HISTORY:

Bath has long been an important pleasure and health resort. Bath buns are one of several distinctive foods which became famous as the town grew during the eighteenth century. The Bath cook and author Martha Bradley (1756) gave a recipe for a Bath seed cake which appears different to other seed cakes in its use of wine and rose water. This instruction came, in fact, from Bradley's lengthy quotation of an earlier household manuscript, possibly dating from the seventeenth century. Elizabeth Raffald (1769) tells how to cook 'Bath Cakes', which are caraway (seed) cakes shaped into buns. The light, yeast-leavened rolls were enriched with cream and butter, but no eggs. Some caraway comfits were worked into the dough and more were strewn over the top. This recipe is repeated in Farley (1783) – a work largely derivative of Raffald – and Henderson (*c.* 1790), a work largely derivative of Farley. When Henderson was re-edited by J.C. Schnebbelie (1804) the title of the recipe was transformed to 'Bath Cakes or Buns'. While Raffald sent her cakes in 'hot for breakfast', Farley, Henderson and Schnebbelie suggested they be eaten at either breakfast or tea. A cookery book produced in the Midlands in 1807

The sun is shining at Stroud Farmers Market. It is shining on four fruit and vegetable stalls, three of them organic, piled high with broad beans; tufted carrots; young beetroot complete with emerald tops; red-skinned potatoes, white-skinned potatoes, yellow potatoes, potatoes blotched pink and white, with their names scrawled on bits of cardboard – Pink Fir Apple, Desiree, Pentland Javelin, Charlotte, Duke of York; shaggy, multifarious salad leaves; onions and shallots; crisp cabbages. It is shining on boxes of white cherries, Merton Glory, blushed down one side, and others of gooseberries as green as opals. It is shining on seven meat stalls, among them offering Gloucester Old Spot and Tamworth pork, Gloucester Long Horn and Hereford beef, Cotswold lamb, free-range chickens from Chepstow and Aylesbury ducklings, and game – rabbit as well as fallow and muntjack venison from the countryside about. It shines on two bread stalls, two cake stalls, two stalls selling apple juice, perry and cider; another with fresh trout, trout pâté and watercress; and on three cheese stalls, one of which has sheeps' milk cheeses coated in ash stacked up like so many small square turrets.

I lurch away up, laden with a couple of chickens from Chepstow, belly pork from Minchinhampton, green back rashers from Dursley, a kilo of carrots from Highrove, kale tops from Wotten, a bag of cherries, a large lump of extra mature Double Gloucester and a Dublin loaf from the WI stall. Second helpings anybody?

Matthew Fort

COOKERY WRITER AND BROADCASTER

calls them Bath buns (Simon, 1960). The proportions are very similar to those in Raffald, except some of the cream is replaced by egg. It, too, deploys caraway, a defining ingredient in these early recipes.

That Bath buns were not universal in the city during the Georgian era may be inferred from the letters of a visitor who never stinted his descriptions of food and drink. John Penrose wrote in 1766 (Penrose, 1983): '...with our Tea Cambridge-Cakes buttered. We have had these too ourselves. They are round thick Cakes, a penny apiece, hardly an Ounce weight; look like Dow [dough], all white and soft: these we toast a little by the fire, just to warm them through, and then butter them; they eat exceedingly well.' Were his Cambridge cakes the forerunners of Bath buns? Jane Austen refers to 'disordering her stomach with Bath bunns' in a letter of 1801 (Austen, 1995).

Meg Dods (1826) included recipes for both Bath cake and Bath buns in her description of English specialities. She likened the dough to the French *brioche* (it included eggs and butter) and suggested caraway seeds for the cake and caraway comfits (sugar-coated) for the buns. Neither cake nor buns were described in the Victorian cookery bibles of Eliza Acton and Isabella Beeton, although the buns occur in Mrs Marshall (1887), retaining their spicing with caraway. The nineteenth century, however, does seem to be the period when Bath buns underwent considerable change and normalization, losing for the most part their distinctive caraway flavour and gaining the now-accepted adornment of nib sugar as well as candied peel or grated citrus zest and dried fruit.

The defining moment appears to have been the Great Exhibition of 1851. The catering contractors served Bath buns in their tens of thousands (David, 1977). This led to the development of a 'Cheap Bath or London bun' described by Kirkland (1907) which was little more than a bun with eggs, orange peel, sultanas and a final ornament of nib sugar. The fat used was lard.

The general move away from caraway is confirmed by Dallas (1877), who suggests a plain brioche dough for Bath buns and Skuse (1892), who advises lemon zest.

In the town of Bath, buns made from a recipe adapted from one dated 1679 are still available. It was used by James Cobb, who founded his bakery in 1866. It does not deploy caraway, except in a residual addition of a pinch of mixed ground spice. The firm of Cobb's continued to trade until the late 1980s, when the business and recipe were acquired by Mountstevens Ltd, who continue to make the buns and have several shops in Bath itself. Beyond the town, it is largely the 'cheap or London' variety that is produced.

TECHNIQUE:

The recipe used by Cobb's was quoted by Grigson (1984). Strong white flour, eggs, butter and crushed lump sugar are used, roughly in the proportions 3:2:1:1, and to the following method. A ferment of yeast, sugar and water is allowed to work for 10 minutes and then eggs and alittle flour are added; this is covered and left for about an hour. The ferment is kneaded with the remaining flour, butter, crushed lump sugar, and a little additional granulated sugar, plus small quantities of lemon juice and mixed spice. It is left to rise, then knocked back and shaped and proved. The buns are baked for 20 minutes at 220°C, glazed with sugar syrup and sprinkled with crushed sugar lumps.

REGION OF PRODUCTION:

South West England, Bath (Somerset).

Bath Oliver

DESCRIPTION:

A round biscuit, 75mm diameter, 3mm thick. Weight: 10g. Colour: pale cream. Flavour and texture: neutral, slightly salty; very crisp. A chocolate-coated version is made, known as a Chocolate Oliver, 40mm diameter, with a thick coating of bitter chocolate.

HISTORY:

Bath Olivers are named for William Oliver, a doctor who was born in Penzance in 1695. He lived most of his life in Bath and was the city's most important practitioner during the time of its greatest expansion. The accepted account is that Dr Oliver created a recipe for thin, palatable, easily digested biscuits, to be eaten by those who came to Bath to take the waters and recover from excessively rich diets. The story continues that Dr Oliver set up his coachman as a baker; providing some premises, 10 bags of flour, £100 and the recipe. This recipe passed by a sort of apostolic succession from Atkins, the original coachman, to Norris, to Carter, to Munday, to Ashman, until it finally came into the possession of Cater, Stoffell & Fortt, who had a shop in Bath until the mid-1960s. The biscuits were always known as Dr Oliver's, then, when in the hands of Fortt, as Original Bath Olivers. Olivers or Bath Olivers were quite possibly a similar biscuit, but not produced by those with the sacred recipe. Nor did they have the distinctive packaging and stamp of the good doctor's head. Although today they come in paper packets with the familiar livery, for many decades they were sold in tall tins.

Although there is this apparently cogent account of an early origin for the biscuits, the earliest reference so far discovered to Olivers is given by Maria Rundell (1807), herself a resident of the city; she gives a recipe which shows them to have been a plain yeast-leavened biscuit. Similar recipes, for example one for 'Bath biscuits' in *The Family Cookery Book* (1812) can be found from the same period.

Law's Grocer's Manual (*c.* 1895) commented that there were several makers of Bath Olivers, and John Kirkland (1907) noted the biscuits were a speciality 'still made in great quantities in Bath, and in which some of the leading houses take great pride'. He observes that there was considerable diversity in the recipes and methods of manufacture, and that the biscuits should be very thin and rich, made with butter only. These statements confirm the biscuits were not as exclusive as legend instructs and cast some doubt on the notion that they were an early version of a health food.

The modern biscuits, still manufactured under the name of Fortt's Original Bath Olivers, but no longer owned by Cater, Stoffell & Fortt, are probably rather different to those known at the beginning of the last century. Various sources agree that they required great care, and possessed distinctive characteristics: they wanted a well-leavened dough, thorough kneading, and were dried in a warm cupboard for 30 minutes, then baked in a slack (cool) oven (Simon, 1960); a special bowed rolling pin was used, so that the biscuits were thinner in the middle than at the edge; there was a singular method for docking (pricking) the dough which required 2 biscuits placed faces together, pricked, and pulled apart again; they should burn a little in the middle during baking 'which is correct for a good Oliver' (Law, *c.* 1895).

The chocolate-coated version has been made since at least the 1960s.

TECHNIQUE:

The recipe used for Fortt's Bath Olivers is a trade secret; the ingredient list shows the biscuits are still yeast-leavened and contain butter; other ingredients are wheat flour, milk, animal fat, salt, malt extract, hops, and an antioxidant (E320). A commercial recipe for craft bakers calls for flour and butter in the ratio 4:1. The flour and butter are rubbed together and made into a stiff dough with milk in which a little sugar and yeast have been dissolved; a little salt is added. They rise for 90 minutes; the dough is kneaded with a brake until smooth; it is rested before being rolled to a thickness of about 3mm and cut into rounds of the appropriate size; these are docked and allowed to rest. They are baked at 190°C until gold and crisp.

REGION OF PRODUCTION:

South England, formerly Bath (Somerset).

Blueberry Pie (Double-Crust Fruit Pie)

DESCRIPTION:

Double-crust pies made with short-crust pastry and a fruit filling are distinct-ively British. Dimensions, flavour and appearance will depend entirely on the maker: whether large or individual pies, cooked on a plate or in a deep dish, in foil

CASINGS, AND SO ON. A WIDE RANGE OF FRUITS MAY BE USED AS FILLING: THE COMMONEST ARE APPLE, ALONE OR COMBINED WITH SPICES, DRIED FRUIT OR BLACKBERRIES; OTHERS, ESPECIALLY RHUBARB, GOOSEBERRIES, PLUMS AND CHERRIES, ARE USED. IN THE NORTH, THIS IS SOMETIMES MADE IN A THINNER VERSION CALLED A 'PLATE PIE', OR IT MAY BE MADE RELATIVELY DEEP AND A THIRD LAYER OF PASTRY ADDED BETWEEN 2 FRUIT LAYERS IN THE FILLING.

HISTORY:

Pies have long been a favourite dish in Britain. The word has been in the language since at least the start of the fourteenth century. There are many recipes and almost any edible item seems at one time or another, to have been put between 2 layers of pastry and baked in the oven. Sweet fruit pies have been known since at least the seventeenth century, when Murrell (1638) gave recipes for 'tarts' of pippins (apples) flavoured with spices, orange zest and rose water; tarts of gooseberries or cherries are also cited. These were similar to modern pies, requiring a double crust, with sugar scattered over the surface before baking.

Fillings varied according to availability of fruit. Apple was probably the most popular; cherries were used in Kent and Buckinghamshire (Mabey, 1978). The blueberry pies now available in Dorset come within this genus of dishes, although their fruit filling is of a more recent tradition, imported in fact from North America (Davidson, 1991). The bilberry (Vaccinium myrtillus) is a bush that grows on acid soils in northern Europe. In Scotland it is known as whinberry (because it grows amidst whin, or gorse) or blaeberry and in Ireland, and in North-East England it is also known as blaeberry (blae means blue). Whortleberries are closely related.

Florence White (1932) records bilberry pies in Yorkshire. Bilberries were available for any-one who cared to pick them in many heathland areas along the south coast, in Wales, the Pennines and in Scotland. Gathering bilberries from the wild is time-consuming and the preserve of enthusiasts; recently, interest in using them as a local speciality in hotels has been rekindled in mid-Wales.

TECHNIQUE:

Short-crust pastry is prepared from flour and fat in the ratio 2:1. Lard is the preferred fat, making a crisp pastry. A mixture of lard and butter is sometimes used to give more flavour whilst retaining the shortness. Fruit is prepared; a portion of pastry is rolled 5mm thick and used to line the pie dish; the fruit, sugar and any other flavourings are placed in this; another disc of pastry is used to cover the top, and the edges are sealed. The top may be sugared or decorated. Pies are baked at 220°C for 10–15 minutes, then at 180°C for 30 minutes.

REGION OF PRODUCTION:

South West England, Dorset, though double-crust pie made with fruit other than blueberries is produced nationwide.

Colston Bun

DESCRIPTION:

A round bun ring marked into 8 wedges; 140mm diameter, 30–40mm deep. Weight: about 250–300g. Colour: golden brown, with a glazed surface, cream interior. Flavour: sweet, with lemon and spice.

HISTORY:

The Colston bun is a popular teabread in Bristol. It is said to have gained its name from Edward Colston (1636–1721), a merchant who made a fortune trading with the West Indies. He founded an almshouse and a school, now a charitable trust administered by the Society of Merchant Venturers. The connection between Colston and the bun is through this trust. Each November, to commemorate the grant of the Charter to the Merchant Venturers, a service is held in the Cathedral attended by the pupils of Colston School. After the service, they are given a small currant bun (called the ha'penny starver), a Colston bun, and a 10 pence piece (the modern British coin based on the old silver florin). Of the 2 buns, it is said the smaller is for the child to consume immediately, and the larger to be taken home to share among the family.

The marked divisions on the top of the bun suggests a connection with the old-fashioned enriched breads known as wigs or whigs, which were also marked in sections. Variant names are Colston ring or ring bun. The ha'penny starver was made with the same dough. They are made today by most craft bakers in the city.

TECHNIQUE:

The recipe calls for flour and butter in the proportions 8:1. The yeast is set to work with sugar and flour in a little warm milk for about 30 minutes; in the meantime, the butter is rubbed into the flour, together with a little sweet spice (cinnamon, allspice and nutmeg), plus grated lemon rind and a little dried fruit and candied peel; then the yeast mixture is stirred in, plus enough warm milk to produce a coherent dough. After rising, shaping, proving and marking, the buns are baked at 220°C for 20–25 minutes. They are glazed with sugar syrup whilst still warm.

REGION OF PRODUCTION:

South West England, Bristol.

Cornish Fairing

DESCRIPTION:

A roughly circular biscuit, 50mm diameter, 7mm thick. Weight: 20g. Colour: dark brown with an irregular, rough surface. Flavour: sweet, distinctly spicy.

HISTORY:

A Cornish fairing is a ginger biscuit of a type long associated with fairs in the South West. Some speculate that the name fairing means a ring-shaped biscuit sold at a fair, but most authorities agree that it actually means objects (not necessarily edible) which could be bought at fairs and were popular as gifts. As we come home with a goldfish in a bowl and candy-floss, so our forebears returned with a little packet of goodies. Florence White (1932) quotes information from Cornwall that 'a proper and complete fairing' included gingerbread biscuits, lamb's tails (caraway dragées), candied angelica, almond comfits and macaroons. Early in the nineteenth century, the poet Keats mentioned the 'gingerbread wives' of Barnstaple (Devon). Recipes for Barnstaple Fair gingerbread are still to be found, even if the sweetmeat itself is no longer available. Almost every fair and festivity in Britain probably had some edible keepsake: in Nottingham it was the cock-on-a-stick, in Bath the gingerbread Valentines, and so on. In more cases than not, the memento was spiced bread, cake or biscuit – the consequence of the medieval love affair with spices. Just the same process can be seen across the water in continental Europe.

The history of the specific biscuits now called Cornish fairing is largely unrecorded. All that is known is that they have been made for many years by a baker's firm called Furniss, which was founded in 1886 in Truro.

TECHNIQUE:

Furniss's recipe is a trade secret. The ingredients include flour, syrup, sugar and shortening (a vegetable fat is now favoured), plus spices and a raising agent. The biscuits are cut with a wire cutter to give a rough surface. Published recipes have flour, butter and sugar in the proportions 2:1:1. The flour is combined with baking powder and bicarbonate of soda, spices – ginger, cinnamon, mixed spice and lemon zest – and granulated sugar. These are bound with a little Golden Syrup to form a coherent dough.

REGION OF PRODUCTION:

SOUTH WEST ENGLAND, CORNWALL.

'He may live without books – what is knowledge but grieving?
He may live without hope – what is hope but deceiving?
He may live without love – what is passion but pining?
But where is the man that can live without dining?'

EDWARD R. BULWER-LYTTON, *'LUCILE'*

Cornish Heavy Cake

DESCRIPTION:

HEAVY CAKE IS A FLAT PASTRY BAKED IN A ROUGH SQUARE ABOUT 10MM THICK, LIGHTLY SWEETENED, WITH CURRANTS IN THE DOUGH. IT HAS A DISTINCTIVE CRISS-CROSS PATTERN CUT IN THE TOP.

HISTORY:

The dialect name 'fuggan' is the one for which the earliest references have been found. It is given in Joseph Wright (1896–1905) attached to quotations dating from the mid-nineteenth century. At this time the word could indicate 3 or 4 different things. Sources agree that these were all based on a heavy pastry: one definition specifies 'a cake made of flour and raisins, often eaten by miners for dinner', which sounds very similar to the modern heavy cake. Alternative versions include cakes with either potatoes in the dough or a slice of pork pressed into the top of the pastry before baking, in which case the dish might also be known as a 'hoggan'.

Nowadays, heavy cake or fuggan seems to refer more to a pastry-like cake containing dried fruit. Recipes vary: one by Dorothy Hartley calls for flour, a little salt and currants, mixed to a paste with clotted cream, rolled out to 20mm thick; another contains flour, sugar, currants and lard; a third is like puff pastry, made with equal quantities of butter and flour (Boyd, 1982). The constants are currants and the criss-cross top. Martin (1993) notes that heavy cake could be quickly made in fishing villages when the boats were seen returning to port, and that the pattern cut in the top was supposed to represent the fishing nets.

TECHNIQUE:

Flour, lard and sugar are used in the proportions 3:2:1, with the same weight of currants as lard. A little candied peel can be added. The flour, salt and sugar are mixed roughly, the lard and currants added. Milk or water may be used to hold the dough together. The dough is rolled out, slashed with a knife and baked at 190°C for 30 minutes.

REGION OF PRODUCTION:

SOUTH WEST ENGLAND, CORNWALL.

Cornish Saffron Cake

DESCRIPTION:

An oblong loaf, 200mm long, 140mm wide, 120mm deep, weighing about 500g. Colour: deep golden crust, speckled with fruit; a pronounced yellow crumb. Flavour: lightly sweetened, slight astringent saffron flavour.

HISTORY:

The use of saffron in sweet breads and buns is now thought typical of Cornwall. Formerly the spice was more widely used in British cookery, and was quite often called for in cakes of the seventeenth and eighteenth centuries (Glasse, 1747). Thereafter, it is found very rarely, although it crops up here and there in recipes collected in Northumberland. Its chief survival was in Cornwall at the other end of the country. It may have lingered here because saffron was still grown. Carolyn Martin (1993) notes that 'various wills and documents refer to "saffron meadows"', and there is a reference to saffron growing at Launcells, near Bude, in the 1870s.

Originally, saffron buns were eaten with clotted cream on Good Friday. The saffron, an expensive spice, is now sometimes replaced with yellow colouring. David (1977) observed that in the past, saffron filaments were infused to produce the colour and they were not strained out before the water was mixed with the other ingredients. She also noted that eggs were not usually added, although the recipe quoted below, collected recently, does include them.

TECHNIQUE:

Recipes for saffron doughs vary in the combinations of spices and dried fruit used. The results are generally light and bread-like. The saffron is mixed into water, which is whisked with a little flour, sugar, whey powder, yeast and eggs. The mixture is allowed to work for 30 minutes. After mixing and bulk fermentation, the dough is scaled off and shaped into buns or loaves. Saffron bread (a variant name for saffron cake) is baked at 175°C: 12 minutes for buns, 30 minutes for cakes.

REGION OF PRODUCTION:

South West England, Cornwall.

Devonshire Split

DESCRIPTION:

A small rounded bun about 80mm diameter, 40mm high. Weight: approximately 40g. Colour and texture: pale gold crust fading to white at lower edge, sprinkled with icing sugar; inside pale, cream crumb; very light bread. Flavour: slightly sweet.

HISTORY:

Cassell's Dictionary of Cookery (1875) defines Devonshire buns as ordinary bun dough using cream instead of milk. The result would have been a soft, light, yet rich dough. The use of split to describe a bun or roll that has been split to receive jam, cream or filling is first recorded in 1905 (*OED*). The reason why these buns carried the alternative name of Chudleighs is unknown. The fact that this small market town in Devonshire was visited by a catastrophic fire in 1807 that started in a bakehouse in Mill Lane is doubtless coincidental. The first reference to this name is in the collections made by Florence White as founder of the English Folk Cookery Association during the 1920s. Here, it is suggested that Chudleighs be rubbed over with butter paper for a gloss, and wrapped in a warm cloth after baking, which gave a soft crust – something found also for Scottish baps. The second record is also in White (1932). White's recipes did not call for cream, only for milk. She also notes the existence of Cornish splits (which were the same but larger) and the alternative name (in Devon and east Cornwall) of tuffs.

The popularity of these buns is reinforced by the tourist industry and the vast quantity of Devon or Cornish cream teas that are served each summer (clotted cream, of course). Most of these may come today with scones, but there are sufficient to keep the Chudleigh living.

TECHNIQUE:

Before the Second World War, small rolls made in Devonshire and

Cornwall, known as splits (or sometimes Chudleighs, in Devon) were yeast-leavened and lightly enriched with a mixture of butter and lard (3lbs flour, 8 ounces butter and 2 ounces lard mixed with water and a little milk). The dough was mixed in a conventional manner, divided into small rounds, proved and baked. On removal from the oven, the hot rolls were rubbed with a butter paper to give them a slight gloss, and covered with a cloth or blanket whilst cooling, giving a soft crust. Sadly, modern practice veers towards the use of margarine and milk powder.

REGION OF PRODUCTION:

SOUTH WEST ENGLAND, DEVON AND CORNWALL.

Dorset Knob

DESCRIPTION:

A DOMED RUSK, 40MM DIAMETER, 35MM HIGH. WEIGHT: ABOUT 10G. COLOUR: PALE GOLD, DARKER ON TOP, A PALER CRUMB. FLAVOUR AND TEXTURE: BREADY, SLIGHTLY SWEET, DRY, VERY CRISP.

HISTORY:

Dorset Knobs (a type of rusk) have been baked by the firm of Moore's since the late nineteenth century. Originally, they are said to have been made from leftover bread dough mixed with butter and sugar and baked in the falling heat of the oven after the bread was removed. It is impossible to say, without further evidence, if the tradition is older than stated. Unlike the similar hollow biscuits made in East Anglia, no surviving domestic recipes have appeared. *Law's Grocer's Manual* (*c.* 1895) merely remarks that there were several species of rusk, mixed from flour, milk, butter and sugar, very light and spongy, cut into 'particular shapes and sizes', first baked on both sides, then dried in a low oven for 3–4 hours.

Around 1939–45, Knobs became the main business of the firm. Today, they make other biscuit specialities. This rusk was sold as a breakfast roll, when it would be dipped in tea to soften; it is also eaten with butter and cheese.

TECHNIQUE:

The exact recipe and method are trade secrets. A dough includes flour, sugar, fat, yeast and water. After kneading and an initial rising, small pieces of dough are nipped off the bulk, shaped and proved for about an hour. They are baked at a high temperature for 20 minutes, turned over and baked a further 10. They are separated by hand, and put in a low oven for 3 hours to desiccate completely.

REGION OF PRODUCTION:

South West England, Bridport (Dorset).

Dough Cake

DESCRIPTION:

A round fruit dough cake – an example bought in Banbury was about 200mm diameter, 50mm deep. Weight: about 500g. Colour: pale brown with a spongy appearance (it is the underside of the cake which is exposed to the buyer) and a few currants showing on the surface; the base (which was the top duringbaking) is smooth, flat and a deeper golden brown; the inside has a fine-textured, off-white crumb, speckled with fruit. Flavour and texture: sweetish, with a slight sourdough taste and a soft, clinging texture.

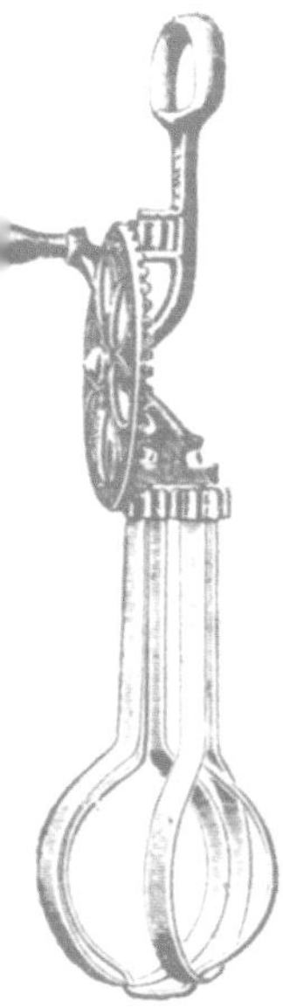

HISTORY:

An early literary reference to the dough cake is dated to the mid-eighteenth century, comes from Devon, and is recorded as a term of affectionate abuse for a thick-headed person (*OED*). This suggests dough cakes were well known, but gives little indication of the recipe. Dough cakes in modern England are similar in composition to lardy cakes, but the added ingredients are evenly distributed through the dough rather than being carefully folded in. A tradition mentioned by Flora Thompson (1939) may have some bearing on this. In rural Oxfordshire, amongst poor households who had no ovens for baking, a 'baker's cake' was made for harvest teas. 'The housewife provided all the ingredients excepting the dough, putting raisins and currants, lard, sugar and spice in a basin which she gave to the baker, who added the dough, made and baked the cake, and returned it, beautifully browned, in his big oven. The charge was the same as that for a loaf of the same size, and the result was delicious.' Since the price of this cake was no more than the cost of the dough, it had to be simpler than lardy cakes which require laborious rolling and folding; presumably the baker simply kneaded the additions through the dough after bulk fermentation, much as today. Dough cakes are made in the same general area as lardy cakes. In Devon, they are most often found on the eastern side of the county. Just over the county border in Dorset may be found the Portland dough cake – described by the WI earlier in the century (Raffael, 1997).

TECHNIQUE:

As with lardy cakes, proportions vary. Cakes made domestically are likely to be richer than those in commerce. A typical baker's recipe would use dough, dried fruit, lard and sugar in the ratio 4:1:1:1. The dough for the cake is removed from a batch for bread after bulk fermentation; the extras are kneaded through; the mixture is scaled off, shaped and placed in tins. Proving times are variable, but can be up to 18 hours. They are baked for 60 minutes at 220°C. After baking, dough cakes are turned out and displayed upside down. The reason for this may be to demonstrate that they are fully cooked or, as with lardy cakes, in consequence of a belief that the lard permeates evenly through the warm cake. Some recipes call for butter, not lard, and some add spices.

REGION OF PRODUCTION:

SOUTH WEST ENGLAND; SOUTH ENGLAND

Easter Biscuit

DESCRIPTION:

A circular biscuit with a fluted edge, 50–90mm diameter, 5mm thick; Weight: 12–20g. Colour: pale gold irregularly flecked with currants. Flavour: sweet, lightly spiced. Short texture.

HISTORY:

In the past, the British made many special foods for Easter, including various breads and biscuits and things like tansy puddings. In the twenty-first century, only hot cross buns and simnel cakes are well-known, but a few others survive. One is the Easter biscuit, known also as Easter cake, in South Western England. Old recipes show them to belong to the same type as Shrewsbury cakes, based on a rich shortbread mixed with currants and flavoured with spices and peel. Harris and Borella (*c.* 1900) say there were many varieties, that they were rather large, cut with a fluted cutter and sugared on top. They give 2 recipes. Firstly, 'the usual', made with butter or margarine and flavoured with oil of lemon; and a 'recommended' one, for which butter and Vostizza currants are specified and lemon zest used to flavour. They comment on a method used by an old-fashioned pastry cook's shop in London where the biscuit was pressed out with the thumbs to give an irregularly shaped biscuit with an uneven surface. The appearance was ugly, but the butter and flavouring of orange and lemon zest made them very good. These recipes are similar to 2 collected by Florence White in the 1930s. One, called a Sedgemoor Easter cake, came from Somerset. According to Bristol baker John Williams, Easter biscuits are still very popular in the city of Bristol and throughout much of the South West; he regards the flavouring of oil of cassia (a form of cinnamon) as the defining characteristic.

TECHNIQUE:

Easter biscuits are a shortbread type. A commercial recipe (*c.* 1925–30) calls for flour, butter, sugar and currants roughly in the proportions 4:2:2:1. They are mixed with eggs and baking powder, nutmeg and oil of cassia. They are baked at 195–205°C until lightly browned. Other recorded recipes may include mixed sweet spice, cinnamon and brandy (Sedgemoor) or lemon zest (London).

REGION OF PRODUCTION:

South West England, Bristol.

Mothering Bun

DESCRIPTION:

A circular bun 90mm across, 30–40mm deep. Weight: 60g. Colour: golden crust, decorated with white glacé icing and a thick coating of hundreds-and-thousands (nonpareils). Flavour: light, slightly enriched bread, with sweet icing.

HISTORY:

Mothering buns are a speciality of Bristol made on the Saturday immediately preceding Mothering Sunday (Mid-Lent Sunday). This is a day on which the Lenten fast was relaxed to allow consumption of richer foods. In the past, it was also associated with the better-known custom of the Simnel Cake. The buns are small and rather plain, and the cakes large, rich and elaborate, although there is evidence for plainer, yeast-raised simnels in various places.

John Williams, a baker who has taken an interest in Bristol specialities, comments that mothering buns have been made for as long as anyone can remember, and that at the beginning of the twentieth century, they were coated with caraway or aniseed comfits, rather than the hundreds-and-thousands now used. This links them to the tradition of Bath buns which once incorporated caraway comfits, and to the many other bun and wig recipes of 200 years ago which used the same flavouring. All bakers in Bristol make mothering buns, only on the Saturday before Mothering Sunday.

TECHNIQUE:

A plain dough is made using flour, fat and sugar in the proportions 10:1:1. A ferment works for about 30 minutes at 32°C. The fat – usually lard, butter is used in particularly rich buns – is rubbed into the flour, sugar and a little salt and the ferment are added. After fermentation, it is knocked back and kneaded again. It is baked at 220°C for 20 minutes. The tops are given a plain icing, followed immediately by dipping in a dish of hundreds-and-thousands.

REGION OF PRODUCTION:

South West England, Bristol.

Oldbury Tart

DESCRIPTION:

A small circular pie about 90mm diameter, 20mm deep. The edge of the pie is nipped into little points, giving a crown effect. Weight: approximately 100g.

HISTORY:

These tarts were also known (more accurately perhaps) as pies. They are distinctive in their use of hot-water pastry, usually associated with savoury pies, in combination with sweet filling. See also Cumnock tarts, below. Gooseberries are the common filling, but black currants are also known. A very similar gooseberry pie was made for Mansfield Fair in Nottinghamshire. No other fruit pies using this type of pastry are mentioned by authorities on British food.

Both the Oldbury and Mansfield pies were noted at the end of the last century. The Nottinghamshire affairs involved melted apple jelly being poured into the warm pies to set as it cooled. This is just like adding jellied stock to savoury pork pies. White (1932) records that the pies were still being sold at Mansfield Fair. Surviving recipes for Oldbury tarts are of more recent date, but the use of brown sugar as a sweetener suggests a tradition stretching well into the nineteenth century before white sugar became cheap and easily available (about 1840). Pauline Gazard, one of the few people who now keeps the dish alive, quotes oral traditions to do with the pies. They should be eaten from the hand, and a good pie is full of juice which runs out when bitten. The pastry should be thin, and the decorative edge is important; there should be 21 points to the crown. They are more difficult to make than ordinary pies, which discourages many. This most interesting tradition appears to be declining. They are still available in small numbers at local fêtes and fairs in July.

TECHNIQUE:

The proportion of flour to fat is slightly more than double the weight. The fat is butter and lard in equal quantities. The dough is made like any other hot-water paste. To shape the cases the dough is rolled out thinly and cut in circles of 160mm diameter. These are hand-raised by pleating the sides 4 or 5 times. They are filled with small gooseberries and soft brown sugar. A pastry lid is nipped with the case to give the pointed effect; a small hole is cut in thecentre. At this stage, the pies are sometimes left to stand overnight, allowing the pastry to firm. They are baked at about 200°C for 25–30 minutes.

REGION OF PRODUCTION:

West England, Gloucestershire.

Sally Lunn

DESCRIPTION:

A low circular loaf; a usual size is about 140mm diameter, about 80mm deep. Weight: approximately 200g. Colour and texture: a deep gold crust on top, fading to cream underneath, with a rich, cream, close-textured, light and melting crumb.

HISTORY:

This light yeast cake is a speciality of the spa town of Bath. There are several theories as to its origin. An early reference in a Bath guidebook of 1780 is to 'a spungy hot roll'. In 1798, they were again said to be hot rolls, 'not long ago in vogue in Bath'. Hot bread was much loved at Bath breakfasts. In 1827 there was an account of how Sally Lunns were named after the girl who cried them for sale ('about thirty years ago'). She and her recipe were adopted and commercialized (*OED*).

There is a charming but probably apocryphal legend that a

Huguenot refugee called Solange Luyon, a name corrupted to Sally Lunn, first made the cakes famous. A building, dating originally from the fifteenth century, is supposed to be the place where she worked. It still houses a restaurant and shop baking Sally Lunns. Bath historian Trevor Fawcett observes that no documentation has ever been produced to support this story.

A completely different hare was started by Eliza Acton (1845). She described her recipe for a 'solimemne' as a 'rich French breakfast cake or Sally Lunn'. Hartley (1954) produced other uses of the word solimemne, variously spelled, and suggests it is a corruption of the French *soleil lune*, sun and moon. In fact, solimemne is a misspelling of *solilem* or *solimeme* which is the name of an enriched brioche from Alsace. The distinguishing feature of *solimemes* (Larousse, 1938) is that they are split horizontally soon after baking, soaked with melted butter which is absorbed by the dough, then reassembled. Whether they made the transition from Alsace to Bath is not known, but maybe the Huguenot has a place. An alternative proposal is that Sally Lunns were discovered by a French chef when travelling in the West Country – Carême is suggested – and he exported the idea to his homeland, where the name was completely garbled into *solimeme.* All this is speculation.

The main characteristics, a light richness derived from a high proportion of eggs and cream or butter in the dough, are consistent through the years. Some recipes are lightly spiced or flavoured with lemon peel. However, Maria Eliza Rundell (1807), herself a resident of Bath, likens a plain but light roll to a Sally Lunn. It is split, whilst still warm, into 2 or 3 horizontal slices and spread with butter or clotted cream, then reassembled for immediate consumption. If more than 24 hours old, the cake is usually toasted before eating.

TECHNIQUE:

The recipe used by the Sally Lunn shop is a trade secret. Other versions are published, for example by David (1977). It calls for flour, cream and eggs in the proportions 2:1:1 and is flavoured with lemon peel.

REGION OF PRODUCTION:

South West England, Bath (Somerset).

Cider (West Country)

DESCRIPTION:

Pale gold-yellow to the eye; some may be cloudy, but much produced com-mercially is usually clarified. Fermented until dry, West-Country cider is robust and astringent with perfumed apple overtones. Typically 6 per cent alcohol by volume.

HISTORY:

Although it must remain uncertain, it does appear that the Anglo-Saxon word *beor* refers to an alcoholic apple-based beverage. In Norman-French dialect, the word *bère* for cider survives to this day. Whether cider existed in early England or not, it is thought the art was stimu-lated by contacts with Normandy after the Conquest, and that cider-making was at first strongest in the South-Eastern counties of Sussex and Kent (Davies, 1993). But there are also many early references to cider in the West Country, including from the 1100s in Gloucestershire and the 1200s in Devon.

Cider from western Britain is distinguished by the use of apples specifically grown for cider-making. This practice has been current for at least 400 years. During the seventeenth century cider became a gentleman's drink, equated with wine. In Herefordshire, much attention was paid to cider apples and methods. Advances at this time included greater selection of apples, refinement of storage and crushing techniques, and the invention of glass bottles strong enough to withstand a secondary fermentation. Celia Fiennes, travelling through Britain in the late seventeenth century, noted the good quality of Hereford cider.

In the eighteenth century cider sank on the social scale: there was increased competition from imported wine; middlemen sold inferior weak brews; and an epidemic of lead poisoning attracted opprobrium (French, 1982). Competition from wine may have been the most influential and long-lasting cause of cider's drop in standing. Cider became a drink associated with the labouring poor; the quality was uneven and the flavour sharp. The juice was mixed with water, giving 'ciderkin' with an alcohol content comparable to that of small beer, a servants' drink. It was this, not the fine ciders of the seventeenth century, that survived. In the late nineteenth century, there was renewed interest. Businesses that are still important today were established. Cider apples were classified according to acidity and tannin content into sweet, bittersweet, and bittersharp. Hereford and Worcester were known for cider made from bittersharps, Devon was known for sweet ciders and Somerset for ciders made from bittersweets (Morgan, 1993). Some of the larger cider-makers established their own orchards.

Advances in knowledge of fermentation, plus expanding urban markets, benefited small factory-based cider-makers but farm production diminished after 1930. English cider generally developed into a consistent, uniform product in which alcoholic strength was considered important (although western cider is generally less strong than that made on the eastern side of the country) and the process was standardized with added yeast cultures.

Since the 1970s, distinct trends have emerged: new planting of orchards of cider apples to better supply the industry; a renewed interest in on-farm cider-making and methods of production. For instance, ciders from single varieties such as Kingston Black, Yarlington Mill, Dabinett, Sweet Coppin and Brown's Apple are now available.

Scrumpy is a name colloquially applied to farmhouse ciders which have been produced by traditional methods, but it has no fixed definition and is frowned upon by cider-lovers. Gloucestershire, Herefordshire and Worcestershire ciders have Protected Designations of Origin (PDO).

TECHNIQUE:

Ciders vary between makers and harvests, as do wines. Methods of production are at heart identical; it is variations in soils, micro-climate and fruit varieties which most affect the flavour. As yet, little systematic attempt to classify these has been made in respect of cider, and the necessary vocabulary is underdeveloped in English.

The hallowed routine followed for making farmhouse cider began with the harvest. The apples were either allowed to fall naturally or were shaken off the tree with a long pole; then they were taken into an apple loft and allowed to mellow. The stored apples of different varieties were blended. They were crushed in a horse-driven stone wheel-mill or, at the end of the nineteenth century, in a powered rotary press. Sometimes the crushed apple pulp (pomace) was left to stand to allow flavour to develop. It would then be pressed. It was placed in 4–6cm layers on hairs, or thick horsehair cloths which were folded over to envelop the pulp, and then built up into a cheese consisting of about 10 filled cloths. Pressure was applied from above by screwing a plate down on to the cheese. In Devon and Dorset, barley straw was used in place of the hairs, but this is no longer practised. As the juice flowed from the press, it was poured into barrels, loosely stoppered, and left to work under the action of naturally present yeasts. Once fermentation had ceased, the cider was racked off the spent yeast.

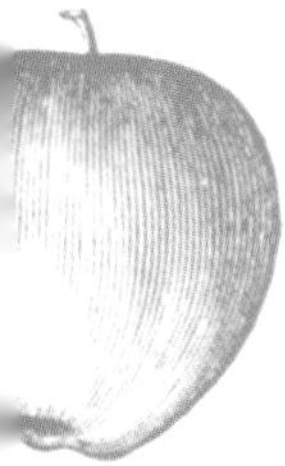

Modern production follows the same sequence but with refinements. The fruit may be dislodged and harvested mechanically. It is blended, picked over and cleaned before mechanical crushing. Hydraulically operated presses, with layers of fruit packed in polypropylene cloths, similar to the old-fashioned screw presses, are used to extract juice by small producers; big horizontal or continuous presses are used for factory operations. The juice may be sterilized with sulphur dioxide and yeast cultures added. Other additions are sugar if the year has been poor, and water by some makers. Fermentation takes place in large vats. The result is generally still, strong and dry. If sweet is required it is usually obtained by adding sugar. Royal cider, where fermentation is stopped by the addition of strong alcohol – which will give a sweeter finish – is not pursued as it used to be in the classic period. Some cider apples have sufficiently well-balanced acid and tannin to produce good cider without further blending. A few makers offer cider produced from single varieties. Otherwise, the apples may be blended before milling or after fermentation. Large companies have turned cider-making into a year-round activity by holding part of the year's apple juice in a concentrated form until required; they may also use concentrated apple juice from abroad.

REGION OF PRODUCTION:

WEST AND SOUTH WEST ENGLAND.

Plymouth Gin

DESCRIPTION:

PLYMOUTH GIN IS COLOURLESS AND TRANSPARENT. ITS FLAVOUR IS AROMATIC WITH CITRUS AND CORIANDER OVERTONES. TWO STRENGTHS ARE AVAILABLE: 37 AND 57 PER CENT ALCOHOL BY VOLUME.

HISTORY:

Gin has been distilled in Plymouth since at least the eighteenth century. Coates, the only company now allowed to use the name Plymouth Gin, began production in 1793 in the building which still houses the distillery. It has continued with little interruption. The 57 per cent spirit was made only for the Royal Navy but a quantity was released to celebrate the bicentenary of the company's foundation. Coates is now marketed by Hiram Walker Agencies, a subsidiary of Allied Lyons.

TECHNIQUE:

A neutral grain alcohol is distilled through a rectifying still to remove odours. This yields a very pure spirit which is 95 per cent alcohol; to this are added the 'botanicals': juniper, coriander seed, orange and lemon peel, angelica, orris root and cardamom. Coates's formula lays greater emphasis on the roots (angelica and orris) than other gins, giving it a distinctive aroma. The mixture is distilled once more in a pot still, checked in a spirit safe, and bottled.

REGION OF PRODUCTION:

South West England.

Shrub

DESCRIPTION:

This is pale gold in colour; its taste is sweet, with citrus and caramel notes. It is 5.3 per cent alcohol by volume.

HISTORY:

The word shrub derives from the Arabic root *sharab*, meaning a sweetened drink. The word and various drinks and confections associated with it are discussed in detail by Alan Davidson (1993). Since the mid-eighteenth century it has been applied to a sweetened drink of rum and oranges, lemons or other acid fruit such as currants. Athough it was clearly old-fashioned by the late 1800s, it was well enough known for *Law's Grocer's Manual* to give a recipe. The taste for it has survived in the South West of Britain, where its manufacture is associated with Bristol. This town carried on an important trade with both the West Indies and the wine- and brandy-producing areas of France and Spain. Rum or cognac were vital ingredients for the drink. The Bristol company that now produces it, J.R. Phillips, makes several other alcoholic cordials, including lovage, peppermint and aniseed.

TECHNIQUE:

The commercial recipe and method are trade secrets, but published recipes state that either brandy or rum can be used as a base. Lemon and orange peel are mixed with the liquor and fresh lemon juice. The mixture is infused for several weeks, it is then sweetened with syrup, strained and bottled.

REGION OF PRODUCTION:

South West England.

Sparkling Cider

DESCRIPTION:

THIS CIDER HAS A STRONG APPLE BOUQUET, WITH THE DRY, SPICY FLAVOUR TYPICAL OF ENGLISH CIDERS. IT IS NORMALLY 5–8 PER CENT ALCOHOL BY VOLUME.

HISTORY:

Sparkling cider was made in Herefordshire in the 1600s. It had been made possible by the development of glass bottles strong enough to withstand the secondary fermentation. Their invention is credited to Sir Kenelm Digby, a man with a deep interest in the arts of brewing and fermenting, whose collection of recipes for food and especially meads, metheglins and other drinks was posthumously published as *The Closet of … Sir Kenelme Digbie, Kt., Opened* (1669). This is a charming myth, for he was a charming man, but the more likely explanation is that Lord Scudamore, whose family was foremost in improving varieties of apples suitable for cider, began to bottle and lay down cider in the reign of Charles I (Davies, 1993). Glass strong enough to hold the explosive liquid was developed as a result of hotter-burning coal furnaces being used by the glassworkers when the use of charcoal was curtailed after 1615. By the end of the century, there was such a trade with London in bottled cider (sent down the Thames from Lechlade) that 5 or 6 glasshouses had been built in the area to supply the bottles.

The tradition suffered in the eighteenth century when cider became the drink of the poor but was revived towards the end of the reign of Queen Victoria. In 1895, *Law's Grocer's Manual* stated that, 'Champagne cider is, or should be, the best mellow or sweet cider bottled before it has fermented or worked much … it is quite frequently made by charging common cider that is deficient in spirit and sparkle with carbonic acid gas.' Over the last century, both secondary fermentation and carbon dioxide have been used by various manufacturers to give sparkling ciders. Since the late 1970s, an increasing interest in the art of making fine cider has led several specialists to experiment once more with sparkling ciders made by secondary fermentation. At least 7 makers produce a naturally sparkling cider.

TECHNIQUE:

A cider produced by the standard English method is used. After initial fermentation, it is allowed to undergo a secondary fermentation in the bottle. A few producers clear the cider by allowing the yeast to settle in the necks of the bottles, freezing them and disgorging it before corking. Others leave the yeast in the bottom of the bottle. Much commercially produced cider is sparkling but it is carbonated.

REGION OF PRODUCTION:

South West England.

Original Urchfont Chilli Mustard

DESCRIPTION:

This grain mustard is dark yellow-orange, with crushed yellow mustard seeds visible and specks of red and dark brown. Its taste is acid, mild mustard with a powerful chilli kick.

HISTORY:

Originally, all mustard must have been fairly coarsely ground. It was only in the early 1700s that the fine, sieved flour now thought of as English mustard became widely known. During the late 1960s, there was a general revival of interest in early recipes and methods for producing various foods. This, combined with a desire to make interesting condiments for meat, led to the invention in 1970 by the Wiltshire Tracklement Company of a whole-grain, chilli-spiced mustard called Urchfont (originally made in Urchfont, Wiltshire). It was the first whole-grain mustard to be marketed in England for many years. Its success led to an expansion of the company's range and its emulation by other small and larger concerns.

TECHNIQUE:

Locally-grown mustard seeds are used. They are blended, ground and mixed and left to stand in drums for up to 14 days (depending on the weather, the colder it is, the longer the process takes). Ingredients: mustard, cider and wine vinegars, black peppercorns, allspice, chillies.

REGION OF PRODUCTION:

South West England, Wiltshire.

Tewkesbury Mustard

DESCRIPTION:

The colour is dull ochre, with coarsely crushed mustard seed and husks visible. Flavour is sharp with a sweet, distinct horseradish aftertaste.

HISTORY:

Tewkesbury Mustard was famous in the 1500s, so famous that it was a byword for a particular kind of stupidity – 'His wit's as thick as Tewkesbury Mustard!' exclaimed Sir John Falstaff in *Henry IV*. The mustard seed was ground in a mortar or crushed with a cannon ball, sifted, combined with an infusion of horseradish, well mixed for at least an hour, made into balls and dried. It was sold and kept until reconstituted with various substances – vinegar, verjuice, cider and red wine are all quoted. No trace of this early industry has remained in Tewkesbury; only the name recalls the association (Man and Weir, 1988).

A habit of mixing horseradish and mustard persisted. References can be found in a recipe by John Nott (1726), and Eliza Acton (1845) gave instructions for making 'Tartar Mustard', a mixture of mustard powder, horseradish vinegar and chilli vinegar. These compounds were made at home, instead of being dried and marketed. Increased interest in the production of speciality foods by small independent producers led to the revival of Tewkesbury mustard in the late twentieth century.

TECHNIQUE:

The ingredients are mustard seed, horseradish root, wine vinegar and acetic acid. The spices are ground, mixed to a paste with the other ingredients and allowed to mature for several days before bottling.

REGION OF PRODUCTION:

West England.

Channel Islands

Jersey Royal Potato

DESCRIPTION:

Jersey Royals are small, kidney-shaped potatoes (they are also called International Kidneys) with a thin white skin and creamy white flesh; they are graded by size into 'ware' or 'mids'. They are a waxy potato with a delicate sweet, earthy taste.

HISTORY:

These potatoes owe their origin to a single seed bought from a local shop by Jersey farmer Hugh de la Haye in 1880. The potato, which had 16 sprouts, was divided up and planted, yielding a good crop of early potatoes. The de la Hayes nurtured the variety until they had enough to trade with. A Jersey newspaper editor, Charles le Feuvre, was responsible for the name 'Royal Jersey Fluke'; the potatoes are now known as Jersey Royals.

A Protected Designation of Origin has been applied for. Marketing of Jersey Royals is intense and tends to exclude the word 'potato' from the name. The aim is to build up brand identity attached to the variety alone. Jersey is well suited to production of early potatoes because of its higher mean temperature. Other districts which have entered the early market are Cornwall and the South-West. Jersey Royals attain a premium price, although there is competition and undercutting from less flavourous tubers from Cyprus and Egypt.

TECHNIQUE:

The seed potatoes are dug and selected in late June. The first shoots are removed, then the roots stored until October. The seed potatoes are arranged by hand, upright in boxes. They are left for about 4 weeks, during which they send out another 3 shoots. Planting is done by hand, sprouting-side uppermost, working from the fields closest to the sea towards the centre of the island. The fields are covered with perforated polythene. Lifting is by mechanical diggers, about 12 weeks after planting; samples are dug daily to ascertain the correct moment. To qualify for the grade of 'mids', they must either be no longer than 45mm prior to a specified date or, after that date, be mechanically graded and be of a diameter not less than 19mm and not more than 32mm.

The fields used for potatoes are mostly dressed with seaweed. Jersey Royals are also grown indoors, hand-graded and packed in oyster kegs holding 5.8kg.

REGION OF PRODUCTION:

Channel Islands, Jersey.

'Though the potato is an excellent root, deserving to be brought into general use, yet it seems not likely that the use of it should ever be normal in the country.'

David Davies, *The Case of the Labourers in Husbandry*

Channel Island Milk and Channel Island Butter

DESCRIPTION:

Channel Island milk is richer in flavour than that of other cattle; Guernsey is slightly yellower in colour than Jersey. Average butterfat content, 5.1 per cent.

Channel Island butter is derived from the churned cream of this milk. Some farm butters bear the traditional decoration of ridges and diamonds produced by using 'scotch hands' (small ridged wooden boards). This butter is also sometimes sold loose. Colour varies with the season: a rich cream in winter, deep cream to gold in summer.

HISTORY:

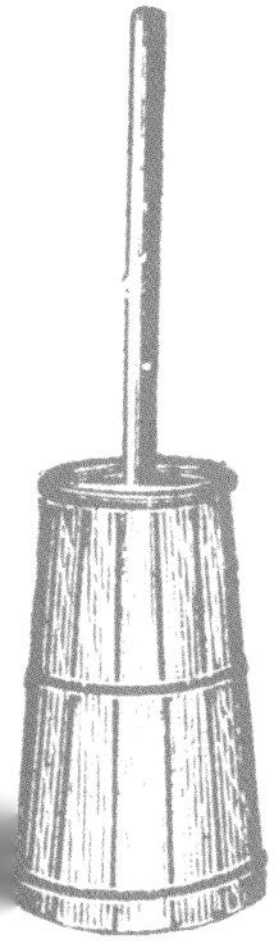

There are 3 breeds associated with Channel Island milk: Guernsey, Jersey, and South Devon. They evolved in the eighteenth century. South Devon cattle are now counted as rare and only one viable dairy herd exists today. The status of Guernsey and Jersey cattle is much stronger. They are exported from their native islands but once they have left, they are not allowed to return. The emphasis on preserving bloodlines on the island means that the milk is derived from the native breeds only. The closure of Jersey to foreign blood dates from 1789, of Guernsey from 1819. The islands exported stock from at least 1724, the annual rate of import into Britain from Jersey running at 2,000 head in 1878. South Devons are associated with Channel Island cattle because of the presence of the gene for haemoglobin B, a characteristic unique to these 3 breeds. There was much crossing of South Devons with Guernseys in the nineteenth century. This may be the route of entry of this genetic identity (Hall & Clutton-Brock, 1989).

Originally known collectively as Alderneys, the cattle have been valued as producers of rich milk for almost 2 centuries. The English aristocracy gave them wide distribution for at first, in the Victorian period, it was a park and home-farm breed associated with country estates (Hall & Clutton-Brock, 1989). The 2 breeds began to develop separately in the mid-nineteenth century, when the Jersey was especially fashionable. On the British mainland, a number of farms maintain herds of pure-bred Channel Island cattle whose milk is marketed separately.

Butter-making is found on the Channel Islands themselves and is undertaken by many owners of mainland British herds, particularly in Cornwall. During 1939–45, milk and butter production was strictly controlled and much on-farm butter-making ceased. The owners of Channel Island cattle formed an association, Quality Milk Producers, shortly after the war, to promote their milk and products made from it. Butter-making using the milk was, and still is, an activity of one major dairy company in the South-West. A number of smaller creameries and dairy farms began producing butter once more in the 1980s, encouraged by moves towards agricultural diversification.

In law, Channel Island milk is defined as milk solely from Jersey and Guernsey herds. 'Gold Top' and 'Breakfast Milk' are brand names registered by Quality Milk Producers in 1956 and 1984 respectively.

TECHNIQUE:

The use of milk from Channel Island cattle is the crucial point in the production of this butter and, because of this, it is collected and processed separately. Theoretically, Guernseys, Jerseys and South Devons can be kept in almost any part of Britain, but they thrive best on rich pastures in the dairying area of the South West (the South Devon, of which there are few, is mostly restricted to this area). For butter, the pasteurized milk is separated mechanically. The cream is usually allowed to ripen; some dairies add a lactic acid starter; it is then churned by conventional English methods. The scale will vary with the producer, from small wooden churns holding a few gallons up to very large stainless-steel industrial units. Small producers prefer to use traditional wooden utensils for working the butter.

REGION OF PRODUCTION:

Channel Islands; herds exist throughout Britain, mainly South.

Guernsey Gâche

DESCRIPTION:

Guernsey gâches (spelled gauche in some English sources) come in various weights, including one of 500g which is shaped like a wide loaf and one of 900g, which is a narrow oblong. Another, named after the maker's shop, the Maison Carré, is set in a shallow oblong tin, above whose edges the dough rises to give a mushroom head. Colour: flaky, golden brown crust, pale yellow crumb with prominent dried fruit and candied peel. Flavour: sweet and rich.

HISTORY:

Guernsey has its own variation on the theme of British fruit breads. J.R. Irons (*c.* 1935) states, 'the one thing they all seemed agreed upon is that it cannot be made without good tough butter' (tough in this instance meaning well-rinsed of water and whey). Recipes show it to be of the enriched dough type which pre-dates the chemically leavened fruit breads now mostly available in Britain. It may be compared to an enriched French brioche. Recipes deriving from eighteenth-century practice have been collected (Cox, 1971). Irons also describes a distinctive shape, certainly universal in the 1930s, stemming from the use of 'flat tins, sides slightly sloping, [which] resembles more the housewife's tin for cooking joints'.

TECHNIQUE:

This bread is heavily enriched: 1 part Guernsey butter, 2 parts sultanas or currants, 2 parts flour. It is yeast-risen.

REGION OF PRODUCTION:

CHANNEL ISLANDS, GUERNSEY.

Black Butter

DESCRIPTION:

A THICK PASTE PACKED IN 500G GLASS JARS; DARK BROWN AND SLIGHTLY GRAINY. SHARPLY APPLE TASTE WITH STRONG LIQUORICE AND CINNAMON NOTES. COMPOSITION: APPLES, CIDER, LEMONS, SPICES.

HISTORY:

Black butter is made on the island of Jersey. Originally a by-product of cider-making, it is a type of apple paste eaten as a spread on bread. The use of the word butter, like 'cheese', is common for these very thick fruit pastes. Butter describes a mixture that is potted, while cheese is the preferred term for a paste poured into an oiled mould to set, then wrapped in paper or foil for storage. Cheese is sliced with a knife and eaten as an accompaniment to dairy cheese or as a sweetmeat on its own. Butter is spreadable.

At first, these were often known as marmalades, the word deriving from the paste made from quince, which is *marmelo* in Portuguese. In Europe it is most often commercialized as *pâte de coings* in France or *membrillo* in Spain.

English recipes for fruit pastes are to be found from the 1400s. Some included spices as well as fruit pulp and honey or sugar. Many fruits have been used as a base: black currants, red currants, elderberries, gooseberries, damsons, quinces and oranges. It was a useful way to cope with seasonal gluts. However, in the nineteenth century, new methods of preserving made them seem old-fashioned and they went out of favour. In the confectionery industry, they survive as fruit pastilles and jellies.

Apples were the most familiar fruit and were reduced to butters more often than to cheeses. The American cookery writer Della Lutes has an evocative description of her family's way with apple butters at the turn of the century. In England, and still today in Jersey, they were called 'black' butters. The novelist Jane Austen wrote in a letter that some black butter served to her was neither properly set nor sweet enough, remarking that it was probably insufficiently boiled.

There has survived on Jersey a tradition, which must stretch back many generations, of making a black butter heavily flavoured with spices. It has remained a communal task and important social event: much labour is needed, both for preparation and for stirring. This has been maintained by a few people, mostly using the exercise as a means of charitable fund-raising. However, production of black butter has declined since the Second World War (Brown, 1986). Interest in the product has lessened. Fewer cider apple trees are now planted and many old ones were uprooted in the storm of October 1987, which affected apple production in general.

TECHNIQUE:

On Jersey, favoured apple varieties include France and Romeril (sweet) and Bramley's (sour). All formulae that survive are for making large batches. One recipe requires 27 barrels of prepared apples, 70 litres of juice, 24 whole lemons, 13kg sugar, 500g cinnamon, 1.5kg mixed spices, 500g nutmeg, plus lemon juice and liquorice. For cooking, a very large, heavy brass cauldron called a *bâchin*, well over a metre in diameter and 30–40cm deep, is needed.

Apples (about 12 parts sweet to 1 part sour) are peeled, cored and cut into small pieces; some are pressed to yield fresh juice. A wood fire is prepared, the *bâchin* put in place and the apple juice first reduced to half by boiling. Three barrels of prepared apples are added and the whole cooked gently. From now on, the mixture must be continuously stirred. Periodically, more fresh apples are added until just over half have been incorporated. Several liquorice sticks (the black dried-juice type) are pounded and added. After the addition of more fresh apple, whole lemons reduced to a pulp are stirred in. Once all the cider apples have been incorporated and cooked down, the Bramley's are added. Cooking continues until the mixture is thought ready for testing; this is done by taking some up on a wooden spoon and slapping it onto a saucer. If the saucer doesn't fall when the spoon is lifted, the butter is deemed ready. Spices, sugar and lemon juice are stirred through. The mixture is potted and sealed. Cooking can take 24–30 hours and the mixture becomes progressively heavy and stiff. Constant, thorough stirring is essential.

REGION OF PRODUCTION:
CHANNEL ISLANDS, JERSEY.

'Hunger is the best sauce in the world.'
MIGUEL DE CERVANTES, *DON QUIXOTE*

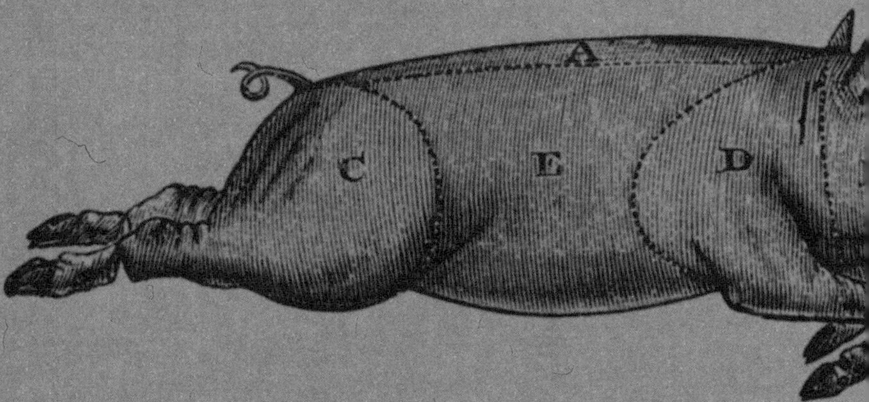
A
C
E
D

Wales

Glamorgan Sausage

DESCRIPTION:

WEIGHT: ABOUT 50G. FORM: MADE IN RISSOLES OR SAUSAGE SHAPES. COLOUR: PALE CREAM-BROWN, WITH WHITE AND GREEN FLECKS. FLAVOUR: CHEESE AND MILD ONION PREDOMINATE.

HISTORY:

Glamorgan sausage is not a meat sausage but a kind of savoury rissole made of cheese, leek or onion, eggs and bread crumbs. The origin is mysterious. George Borrow (1862) mentioned eating them for breakfast, and remarked that he thought them 'not a whit inferior to those of Epping', which could indicate either that he ate a meat sausage comparable with those of Epping, near London, or that he ate a meatless sausage and was pleasantly surprised by it. Epping sausages were skinless, like those from Oxford, and coated with egg and crumbs (Freeman, 1996).

Perhaps the use of cheese in savouries such as 'rabbits', made by melting cheese with flavourings, was a habit inherent in Welsh cookery – it speedily transferred to this meatless sausage. Glamorgan sausages were probably a dish of domestic cookery until recently, if they existed at all. One theory scouted is that they were developed in response to the meat shortages of the Second World War. After their moment of Victorian fame, they are little recorded until the mid-twentieth century, when Dorothy Hartley (1954) gave the recipe which is essentially that still used.

TECHNIQUE:

The main ingredients are bread crumbs and cheese, in the ratio of approximately 2:1; a little finely chopped leek or onion, a pinch of mixed herbs, a little mustard powder, plus salt and pepper are bound with egg yolk; the mixture is divided into portions and rolled on a floured board before frying.

REGION OF PRODUCTION:

South Wales.

Laverbread

DESCRIPTION:

Laverbread is a dark greenish-brown purée. For sale it is wrapped in clear Cellophane to make packs of about 200–250g; the fresh seaweed from which it is produced has purplish fronds and is attached to rocks on the seashore below the high tide mark. Flavour: gelatinous texture, faint iodine-sea taste.

HISTORY:

Laverbread is the common name for *Porphyra umbilicalis*, a type of seaweed common on the shores of western Britain. It is associated with the food habits of South Wales and is eaten to a lesser extent in north Devon and Scotland.

Florence White (1932) discussed laver as a speciality of Devonshire, Somerset and Wales. She noted that it was well known in London 'before the invasion of French chefs in 1848', although consumption had declined by the end of the century. She mentions it was packed in earthenware pots for transport from Watchet in Somerset in 1797, and that it 'is prepared at the place where it is gathered, Braunton in particular is one'. Theodora Fitzgibbon (1965) observed that it was also known in Bath during the eighteenth century, where it was sold in little china pots.

The Welsh have the most persistent tradition of laver gathering and eating. It is known there as *bara lawr*, *llafan*, *menyn y môr*. 'In the eighteenth and nineteenth centuries, women living in the coastal regions of Anglesey, Glamorgan and Pembrokeshire were ardent gatherers of laver,' it was a trade pursued strictly by low-income families (Tibbot,

1986). Mabey (1978) also commented on this well-organized trade, 'with large drying houses built along the shore, where the weed was cured so that it would keep well'. Glamorgan and Pembroke are now the most important areas of production. In fact the supplies of the raw material are becoming scanty in South Wales and Scottish seaweed is brought down for processing (Davidson, 1979). A little gathering is still carried on for consumption in Scotland where the Gaelic words *slouk* and *sloke* describe the same plant. There is some evidence (Evans, 1995) that it is still gathered between Clovelly and Westward Ho! on the north Devon coast.

In Wales, laver is mixed with oatmeal and fried in bacon fat for breakfast. Laver heated with butter and the juice of Seville oranges was a classic Victorian sauce for roast mutton.

TECHNIQUE:

Laverbread is gathered from the rocks at low tide. It is gathered at any time of the year, but storms and changes in the level of sand around the rocks can make the harvest difficult. It is washed many times – in 7 lots of water – to remove any sand and grit, then steeped in fresh water to reduce saltiness, with a little bicarbonate of soda added to counteract any bitterness. The fronds are stewed in their own moisture for up to 7 hours until they become a soft purée. The excess water is drained off; the laverbread is now ready for sale and finishing at home as required. According to Welsh food expert Gilli Davies, it is collected daily and boiled in small, family-run factories; it is sold from market stalls and travelling fish vans. A small quantity is canned, principally for export.

REGION OF PRODUCTION:

South Wales.

Caerphilly Cheese

DESCRIPTION:

Pressed cow's milk cheese. Caerphilly cheeses are made in a wheel or millstone shape, a flat cylinder which is shallow in proportion to its diameter. This was about 18cm diameter

AND 6CM HIGH; SIZES ARE NOW VARIABLE ACCORDING TO WEIGHT, WHICH IS GENERALLY IN THE RANGE 400G–4KG. COLOUR: WHITE. FLAVOUR AND TEXTURE: ACIDIC, WITH SLIGHT LEMON NOTE AND A FLAKY TEXTURE.

HISTORY:

Caerphilly is a town which has given its name to the only Welsh cheese which has become well known outside the Principality. Other cheeses were made in Wales in the past. Rance (1982) speculated that Caerphilly cheese supplanted an earlier type from a region known as Eppynt, which was a similar shape but was kept for 2–6 months before being eaten. He states that Caerphilly cheese, 'was widely available for Welsh miners from the farms of Glamorgan and Monmouth between the early 1800s and 1914', and that small-scale farm cheese production seems to have been common. Demand began to exceed supply with the growth of cities during the 1800s.

Since that time, the cheese has also been associated with Somerset. Caerphilly, a small cheese intended to be eaten young, offered commercial advantages over Cheddar, which requires months to mature. Somerset Caerphilly was sold at Highbridge market, whence much was exported to Wales.

Under terms imposed by the Ministry of Food during 1939–45, production ceased as it was not long-keeping. When it resumed, in Wales it was concentrated in creameries. Some farm production continued in Somerset, where it is made to this day. Traditional farmhouse methods at about the time of the First World War were recalled by Arthur Jones in an article written in the 1950s. Recently, Caerphilly has been revived in South Wales, where it is now produced on several farms. Occasionally, an aged Caerphilly is available from cheese shops.

TECHNIQUE:

Craft method: 1–2 per cent starter is added and the temperature gradually raised from 21 to 31°C; then it is renneted and cut into 5mm cubes. It is stirred for 15 minutes. Stirring continues as the temperature of the curd is raised to about 33°C and the particles break cleanly without being soft in the centres. Then the curd is allowed to settle in the whey for 10–15 minutes before the vat is drained. After the whey has run off, the curd is cut and piled into half-cone-shaped masses, then cut in wedges and piled at the back of the vat. The curd is cut into 2.5cm cubes, salted, and put into moulds. It is lightly pressed for about 18 hours, then brined for 24 hours and kept 4–5 days.

Creamery production is a similar process up to the stage at which the whey is drained; then the curd is cut and piled along the sides of the vat in a smooth bank, gradually draining the whey and allowing the acidity to develop for the next stage. The curd is passed through the mill once, salted, and packed into moulds. Pressing, brining and ripening are carried out in a similar manner to craft production. Caerphilly is available all the year.

REGION OF PRODUCTION:

South Wales; South West England.

Cockle (Penclawdd)

DESCRIPTION:

The legal minimum size was regulated in 1959 to 20mm across. They are sold raw in their shells or cooked and shelled, by weight or volume measure. Colour: the shells vary from yellow (from the low tide mark), through grey, to orange and grey with black patches (from the high tide mark). Flavour: considered to be amongst the best-flavoured cockles fished around the British coast; when fresh, they are very sweet and succulent.

HISTORY:

Cockles (*Cardium edule*) were important in the Welsh diet. The gathering of shellfish developed into a commercial enterprise as the population of South Wales increased during the industrial revolution (Jenkins, 1977). The Victorians appreciated fully the value of the cockle fisheries in South Wales, including Penclawdd, a village on the

Burry estuary on the north side of the Gower Peninsula. The freshly dredged cockles were boiled in the open air, placed over the fire in large pans with a little water. The liquor was reserved and used for washing the batches, after riddling to remove the shells from the flesh. Finally they were washed in fresh spring water and placed in baskets or wooden tubs. Women took the cockles to market in Swansea on the train, carrying the containers on their heads. Jenkins cites living memories of them waiting at the station, dressed in Welsh costume, their baskets covered with white cloths. Until the 1920s, donkeys were used for transport on the beach, the sacks of cockles hung like panniers. Horse-drawn carts with a higher carrying capacity replaced them about the time of the World War II. Horse transport ceased in 1987, replaced by tractors and Landrovers.

In the post-war years, the fishery has been strictly regulated as a conservation measure. The number of people involved has declined from over 200 in 1900–10 to less than 50 in 1970–77. Several reasons are postulated, including pollution, natural variations in the course of rivers, over-fishing and changes in foreshore vegetation. Cocklers also believe that oyster-catchers eat many of the shellfish, and that cockles migrate. A cockle fair takes place in Swansea Market every September.

Today cockles are eaten freshly cooked and seasoned with white pepper and vinegar, made into pies with bacon, dipped in batter and deep-fried, or used in soup. The form in which most landlocked British consumers encounter them is pickled in vinegar.

TECHNIQUE:

Penclawdd is on a river estuary known as Burry inlet. It is the best known of several villages whose inhabitants collect shellfish from wide sands on either side of the estuary; the relative importance of these beaches varies according to changes in the course of the river. The cocklers observe and test the beds carefully for years before deciding which ones to work. They work with the ebbing tide, using a small knife with a curved blade to scrape the sand and expose the cockles, which are drawn together with a rake, and then riddled to separate those which are too small. After washing in pools on the beach, the shellfish are loaded into sacks. The best cockles are considered to come from sandy stretches of beach. They may be sold uncooked in their shells, or boiled and shelled. The method of cooking is to steam the shellfish in perforated baskets for 6–7 minutes, sieve them, and wash the meats in fresh water. Hygiene regulations now being introduced demand that the cockles be cooked for a specified time at a temperature no lower than 98°C; the process is recorded on a continuous read-out. Two methods are being experimented with to achieve this: the use of a steam-jacketed cooking pan; and the use of a continuous belt which carries the washed, shell-on cockles through hot water for 4 minutes, before shaking the cooked meats free into a salt bath (which allows for separation of grit), after which they are washed in cold water.

REGION OF PRODUCTION:

South Wales.

Mussel (Wales)

DESCRIPTION:

Minimum length is 50mm; the cultivated mussels are reliably fattened and well-flavoured.

HISTORY:

Fisheries for mussels are found on the East, South and West coasts of Britain. In North Wales, a mussel fishery was recorded in the River Conway in the eleventh century. Mussels are still fished there today from naturally-occurring beds, and a much bigger fishery has developed in the Menai Straits, to the South West.

TECHNIQUE:

In North Wales, a small-scale fishery is pursued by hand methods using rakes and small boats to harvest the natural mussel bed of the Conway estuary. Larger-scale mussel farming, using mussel seed collected from the Irish Sea littoral is centred on Bangor. The mussels are fattened in lays, and harvested by dredging.

REGION OF PRODUCTION:

North Wales, Conway (Gwynedd).

Sewin

DESCRIPTION:

Sewin weigh 750g–9kg. In Wales, fishermen divide the sizes into 3 categories: under 900g, they are known as a shinglin; 900–1400g, they are twlpyn; and from 1400g up to 9kg, they are called gwencyn. The skin of sewin is grey on the back, silver-white on the belly and an evenly distributed pattern of black flecks over the sides and back; the flesh is a light pink. It has a delicate, rich flavour. Sewin taken in nets are always in excellent condition, with firm flesh.

HISTORY:

Sewin, sea trout or salmon trout, is *Salmo trutta*, a member of the brown trout family. It is a freshwater fish which spends part of its life cycle at sea. Wales is not the only part of the British Isles in which it is caught, but certain rivers there have a reputation for being rich in these fish. The rivers Teifi, Dyfi and Conway have long been important for catching sewin, the Teifi in particular. The river Taff was noted for its abundance of sewin in the early 1800s.

It is probable that sewin have been taken from Welsh rivers for as long as there have been human inhabitants. A few fishermen carry on interesting methods of catching them. J. Geraint Jenkins (1971) discussed these in detail, noting that they are of ancient origin. Most notable is the net held between 2 coracles, a craft thought to have been used for thousands of years in Britain. Coracle fishing is fast disappearing; the craft requires skilful handling and they have been discouraged by those responsible for fishing rights. Coracle men once had a reputation for poaching: the boats were noiseless, difficult to see at night and easily portable to the pools where salmon congregate.

Fishing licences are also expensive for coracle operators. There is now much competition from leisure anglers – a growing breed. The fish population has also been affected by the building of hydro-electric dams and by fungal disease. Further restrictions are proposed on the season the coracles are allowed to fish and the number of licences issued. Sewin are caught between the beginning of May and the second week in June and coracle fishing in general is limited to 1 March to 1 September. Despite all this, the tradition survives, although the men express doubts about the future.

The fish, of course, is caught in other rivers in Britain and Europe. The link to this region of Wales is in the manner of fishing. There is a recipe that has been christened after the river of origin: Teifi sauce, made from fish stock, port, anchovy, mushroom ketchup and butter, reduced to a strong liquor. This is a frequent accompaniment, although trout are often eaten with nothing more complicated than boiled new potatoes and fresh peas.

TECHNIQUE:

Coracles and nets are used either at night or when the rivers are in spate. The fishermen operate in pairs, each one in his own coracle. Boats move downstream with the current, to catch the fish as they swim upstream. One man is recognized as the senior; he gives orders, hauls in the net, and kills any sewin or salmon caught by clubbing the fish. The partner is usually a son or younger brother; he always occupies the coracle on the right-hand side of the river as the boats move downstream. They continue for a mile or more; once the end of the trawl is reached, the boats are carried on the fishermen's backs to the start once more, for as many passes as are deemed suitable.

Formerly, the rivers were divided into sections, each corresponding to the fishing rights of a particular village. Apart from coracles and nets, hand nets are also used in estuaries, and weirs and basket traps in the rivers. The details of construction vary from river to river.

REGION OF PRODUCTION:

South Wales, Dyfed.

Welsh Bacon

DESCRIPTION:

Unsmoked cured pork for cooking. Sides measure 50–60cm long, 30–40cm wide, 3–5cm thick; a medium side weighs about 7kg. Colour: thin, dark red streaks of lean, in a white fat layer 3–4cm deep; the outsides are powdered with dry salt. Flavour: very salty, with good cured pork flavour.

HISTORY:

Archaeological sites in Wales yield a higher proportion of pig bones than of any other domestic animal, but improved breeds are not identifiable until the 1800s. The Welsh pig, known in the 1920s as Old Glamorgan, has indeed become a useful commercial strain. There was much keeping of house pigs – in both town and country – fed on waste and whey or buttermilk and fattened on barley. Home-cured bacon was common until the 1950s. The distinctive features of Welsh bacon, the fat and salt, would not have been so remarkable in the past. It was generally considered desirable for pigs to be very fat, and a heavy salt cure was employed to ensure preservation when control of hygiene and temperature were less than certain. The development of lighter cures, demands for leaner meat, worries about the consumption of saturated fat and the death of the tradition of home curing have led to the disappearance of this type of bacon except in West Wales, where it is still much favoured. The meatier back bacon, cut from the loin, can be grilled or fried, or used in cawl (Welsh broth). The fattier part is better employed as a source of fat, salt and flavour for cooking vegetables, especially leeks and potatoes. Several examples of this type of dish are known in Welsh cookery. Bacon fat is the customary medium for heating laverbread.

TECHNIQUE:

Pigs are selected for weight; the largest are favoured. Specific breeds are not sought. After slaughter, the sides are cut: for Welsh bacon, these do not include either the shoulder or the leg, they consist of the loin and attached belly only. They are placed in a bed of dry salt plus a very small proportion of saltpetre. The mixture is rubbed in by hand once every 1 or 2 days for 3 weeks. The sides are hung to dry for about 14 days. Before sale, they are divided longitudinally into a short back piece containing the lean and a longer streaky portion, which is very fatty. These can be further cut into rashers if required. Some makers roll the sides, in which case they are boned before salting and rolled afterwards.

REGION OF PRODUCTION:

South Wales, Dyfed.

COMPARE WITH:

Wiltshire Bacon, South West England (p. 43.)

Welsh Black Cattle

DESCRIPTION:

A deep, rich red lean, with white fat. Tender, well-marbled but otherwiserelatively lean; excellent flavour.

HISTORY:

The forerunners of the Welsh Black were known to the graziers and butchers attending the cattle fairs of the Midlands and London as 'Welsh Runts' and were admired for their hardiness. As a mountain breed, they were small and thin to begin with; during the long journey to the English fairs (including, for the animals reared on the island of Anglesey, a swim across the Menai Straits) they became even more emaciated. However, as early as 1695, the ability of Welsh runts to do well on good pasture – for instance Romney Marsh, in Kent – was noted. The beef from such animals was much admired; in 1747 Hannah Glasse recommended Scotch or Welsh beef for making beef hams, a recipe which required 'the leg of a fat but small beef'. Youatt (1834) described Welsh cattle as very fair milkers with a propensity to fatten. He thought the beef equal to that of Scottish cattle, that they would live where others starved, and that they found a ready sale with London graziers and butchers who were rarely disappointed, despite the apparently poor appearance of the animals on arrival.

Two breed societies were established at first but they amalgamated in 1904. The cattle were recognized as a dual-purpose breed up to the 1970s, popular as milk animals with those who require a small supply for the family. Today they are recognised primarily as Wales' only native Beef Breed. About 700 pedigree herds are now registered in the United Kingdom and the breed is also strong in Canada, New Zealand, Australia and Europe.

TECHNIQUE:

The emphasis in commercial herds has been on beef production and consequently the animals have become larger and their conformation has altered in favour of this use. They are grass-fed for much of the year, but housed in late winter and fed on silage, hay and, in some cases, locally produced barley. Those cattle destined for beef are killed at 18–24 months.

REGION OF PRODUCTION:

WALES.

Welsh Ham

DESCRIPTION:

A CURED, UNCOOKED HAM WEIGHING UP TO 22KG. THE EXTERIOR OF A WHOLE RAW HAM DISPLAYS DARK BROWN-RED LEAN AND YELLOW FAT, COVERED BY GOLD-BROWN SKIN. WHEN SLICED, THE LEAN IS A DEEP TRANSLUCENT ROSE-PINK TO DARK RED, WITH WHITE FAT; ON COOKING IT BECOMES AN OPAQUE, PALER PINK. FLAVOUR: A WELL-SALTED HAM, WITH DISTINCT SWEET PORK FLAVOUR.

HISTORY:

Ham curing in Wales is largely undocumented but the importance of pig meat in the Welsh diet is long established (Wilson, 1973). In the seventeenth and eighteenth centuries, Welsh hams were often made from sheep meat, but no survivals of this can now be found. Like the English, Welsh farmers killed their own pigs and cured the meat for ham and bacon (Webb, *c.* 1930). Albert Rees, the company now

Over the past year I've been busy travelling around the British Isles to search out the best of British produce and producers with a view to restoring our culinary heritage and as part of my new book, *British Regional Food.* In fact, *The Taste of Britain* was a part of my inspiration. For me, Wales held lots of delicious surprises and although laverbread wasn't one of them as I'd had it before, I had forgotten just how good it was. Laverbread has lots of possibilities – it can even be spread on toast! – but I think one of my favourites is when it's served simply with rashers of cured bacon.

Bacon Chop with Laverbread

4 thick bacon chops (each weighing about 120-150g – on the bone, they will be heavier), cured or smoked on the bone or 4 thick rashers of bacon
200-250g laverbread
salt

Preheat grill or griddle pan and cook the bacon chops for four-five minutes on each side. Meanwhile, put the laverbread into a pan with a knob of butter and gently reheat. Spoon the laverbread on to four serving plates, with a bacon chop on each.

Mark Hix

Columnist, author, and Chef Director of Le Caprice, The Ivy and J. Sheekey, London producing Welsh hams and Carmarthen hams, evolved from the country habit of selling produce such as butter and hams in the local markets. The founder's mother took home-cured bacon and hams to the local towns and the present company was founded in 1962 to sell Welsh hams and dry-cure bacon in the markets of South Wales. The dry-cure Welsh hams were always eaten cooked; from these, the uncooked Carmarthen hams have evolved to suit modern taste for something designed to be cut into very thin slices to eat raw.

TECHNIQUE:

Hams from large pigs are preferred; they are selected by weight rather than breed. The hams are removed from the carcass and left square-cut. They are placed in a bed of dry salt with a very small proportion of saltpetre; this is rubbed in several times a week for 6 weeks. Welsh hams are dried and matured for 3 months. Carmarthen hams are kept and matured for another 3–6 months.

REGION OF PRODUCTION:

SOUTH WALES, CARMARTHEN.

Welsh Mountain Sheep

DESCRIPTION:

DRESSED CARCASS WEIGHT VARIES FROM 10KG (FOR VERY SMALL, MOUNTAIN-BRED LAMB) TO ABOUT 19KG (FOR THE LARGEST LAMBS OF THESE BREEDS, GROWN AT A LOWER ALTITUDE). AN EXCELLENT SWEET, NUTTY FLAVOUR, VERY TENDER AND RELATIVELY LEAN.

HISTORY:

The various Welsh Mountain and Hill sheep breeds evolved in a harsh environment whose climate is cold and wet. Don Thomas of Welsh Lamb Enterprise remarks that, from the late seventeenth century, the excellent flavour of the lamb was praised and attributed to the mixture of heather, herbs and grass that formed their diet. In the mid-nineteenth century, George Borrow wrote ecstatic lines about the small, tender, aromatic leg of Welsh mutton on which he dined, celebrating the herb-rich pastures of the area where the sheep were reared. The reputation of Welsh Mountain breeds for tender, sweet meat has grown since then. The inclusion of the word Mountain in the titles of the various breeds indicates the animals have been selected over the years to tolerate a difficult climate and poor pastures. Other characteristics, such as speckled or striped faces and the colour of the wool, have been dictated by a desire to breed more ornamental animals. The meat from the various breeds shares general elements of size, flavour and tenderness. There are a number of breeds recognized as Welsh Mountain: Black Welsh Mountain; South Wales Mountain; Welsh Mountain Badger Face; Welsh Mountain Hill Flock; Welsh Mountain Pedigree. They are each represented by their breed societies. At slightly lower levels, the hill breeds Kerry Hill, Hill Radnor, Beulah Speckled Face, and Welsh Hill Speckled Face all produce lamb which has a good flavour but on somewhat larger carcasses.

TECHNIQUE:

Welsh Mountain breeds are reared on old-established pastures at altitudes of 200 metres or more. These are herb-rich, and receive little fertilizer; some production also takes place on ley pasture at lower levels. The sheep are tough, hardy and self-reliant. Several breeds have exceptional resistance to health problems. Lambing is between mid-February and late April, depending on the altitude. Lambs remain with their mothers until fully weaned and then are finished slowly on mountain grazing. The short lambing season and the lack of winter grazing mean that most of the pure-bred lambs are killed in early and mid-autumn.

Welsh Mountain sheep are also much used in the stratified system of lamb production. The ewes produce cross-bred lambs with lowland sires (often one of the Leicester breeds); the progeny are known as Welsh Halfbreds or Mules, depending on the exact parentage. In turn, the ewes from this generation, pastured in the valleys, produce lambs destined entirely for the meat trade, using meat breeds (traditionally Suffolks) as sires. This system, typical of all highland regions of Britain, utilizing breeds traditional to those areas, produces various sizes and flavours of lamb, destined for specific markets within the country.

REGION OF PRODUCTION:

WALES.

Aberffraw Cake

DESCRIPTION:

A THIN, SHELL-SHAPED BISCUIT, 70MM DIAMETER, 3–4MM THICK. WEIGHT: ABOUT 14G. COLOUR: PALE GOLD. FLAVOUR: RICH, BUTTERY, SWEET.

HISTORY:

Aberffraw or Aberfrau, from which these cakes take their name (they are called, in Welsh, *teisen Berffro*), is a village on an estuary in the south of Anglesey. It was once upon a time (in the twelfth century) the seat of the Eisteddfod. Another name for these biscuits is *cacen* [cakes] *Jago*, i.e. St James's cakes, recalling their distinctive shape of a scallop shell, the emblem of pilgrims to Santiago de Compostela in Spain (Freeman, 1980). The shape was obtained from shells of the small queen scallops readily found on the shore near Aberfrau.

The earliest known reference is Cassell's (1896). They have since appeared from time to time in collections of regional recipes. Recipes are of 2 types: a shortbread composed of flour, butter and sugar; or one based on a Victoria sponge which includes these ingredients plus eggs. Until recently they were made occasionally by local bakers, but are now a rarity. Joan Griffiths, who still makes them in North Wales, uses a recipe inherited from her mother-in-law, who came from the Aberffraw area.

TECHNIQUE:

The recipe most frequently cited is a shortbread of flour, butter and caster sugar in the proportions 4:3:2. The butter is rubbed into the flour until fine crumbs, then the sugar stirred in. The method of shaping is to take a knob of the mixture and press it over the underside of a sugar-sprinkled scallop shell to give a thin, fan-shaped biscuit.

Alternatively, the mixture can be shaped into a long roll, chilled, and sliced; lines are marked on top to imitate the shell markings. The cake-type recipes state that the mixture should be spooned into a greased shell as if into a patty tin. They are baked at 190°C for 5–10 minutes. The cakes should not brown; they become crisp as they cool.

REGION OF PRODUCTION:

North Wales, Anglesey.

Bara Brith

DESCRIPTION:

Bara Brith is generally baked in a loaf shape. One weighing 400g measures approximately 70mm wide, 140mm long, 90mm deep. The crust is golden brown. Commercial versions often use white flour and sugar, giving a pale gold-beige crumb speckled with fruit. Soft brown sugar gives a darker crumb. The outside of the loaf is sticky with a transparent sugar glaze. Flavour: slightly sweet and spiced.

HISTORY:

The name in Welsh means speckled bread. It shares a common origin with other British spiced and fruited loaves. No early references have been located; oral tradition shows that such breads, known as *teisen dorth* in South Wales and *bara brith* in the north have been known since the early twentieth century (Tibbott, 1976). Originally they were based on leftover bread dough, but eventually a separate recipe evolved. The North Wales name became more general in the middle of the century, and is now used almost exclusively.

TECHNIQUE:

There are many recipes for this bread, which should be yeast-raised, although chemical agents are frequently substituted. At first, lard was the accepted shortening and whey the liquid. Butter or margarine and milk are now used. Otherwise, the essentials are a light enrichment of butter and sugar, dried fruit and candied peel, and a flavouring of

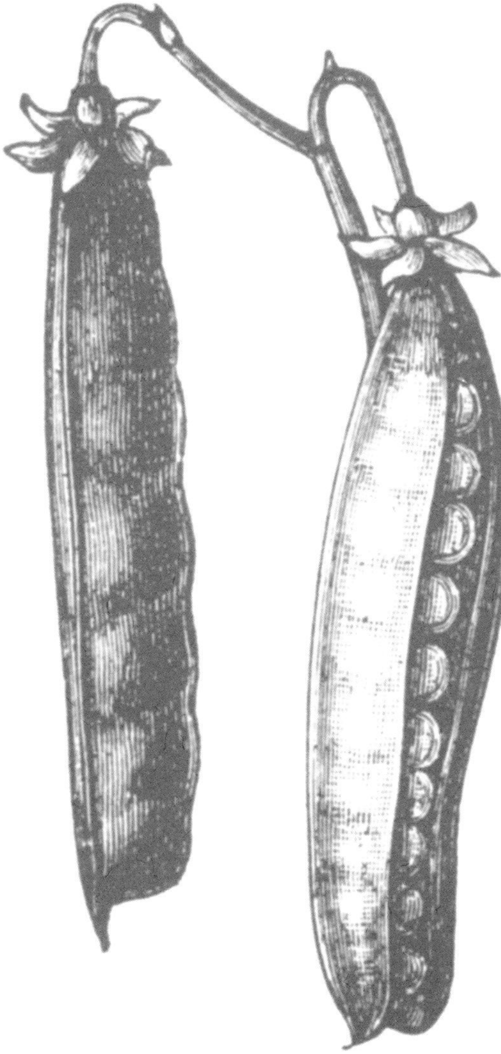

'Part of the secret of success in life is to eat what you like and let the food fight it out inside.'

Mark Twain

mixed sweet spices. Eggs are sometimes, but not always, included. After fermentation, shaping and proof, it is baked at 210°C for 60 minutes. Most commercial bakers produce the bread.

REGION OF PRODUCTION:

WALES.

Bara Planc

DESCRIPTION:

A THICK, GRIDDLE-BAKED DISC, FLATTENED TOP AND BOTTOM, SLIGHTLY BOWED AT THE SIDES, IN 2 SIZES, 100MM DIAMETER, 40MM THICK OR 140MM DIAMETER, 60MM THICK. WEIGHT: 300G (SMALL), 450G (LARGE). COLOUR AND TEXTURE: BROWN ON TOP AND BOTTOM, DARKER IN IRREGULAR PATCHES, DEEP CREASES SHOWING WHERE THE DOUGH HAS BEEN ROUGHLY PRESSED TOGETHER, A WHITE BAND AROUND THE MIDDLE; WHEN CUT, THE SECTION SHOWS A CRUMB WHICH IS RELATIVELY OPEN IMMEDIATELY INSIDE THE CRUST, BUT BECOMES PROGRESSIVELY CLOSER TOWARDS THE MIDDLE; DENSE-TEXTURED BREAD, CONTAINING VERY LITTLE SALT; THE CRUST IS CHEWY.

HISTORY:

The Welsh means griddle-bread. How long these thick, round loaves have been made in the industrial towns along the Glamorgan coast is unknown. This is an area of heavy industry, which had a large and impoverished working population. Enclosed ovens were uncommon in the houses of the poor until the mid-twentieth century. Griddle baking was the usual method for cooking all sorts of breads, cakes and pastries. It is impossible to say if they are an evolution of an older, rural bread (possibly including barley or oats), or a type which developed separately when cheap roller-milled wheat flour became available. Recipes are often quoted in collections, such as *Farmhouse Fare* (1963). Jan Whitehouse, whose family have been bakers in Swansea for more than 100 years, states they have been made for as long as any present-day inhabitants can remember.

TECHNIQUE:

The recipe is very plain, using white flour, a little lard, milk and water. The raising agent is yeast. Once mixed and risen, the dough is knocked back and moulded roughly into a large cake. The thickness should be no more than 40–60mm. After a final proof of 15 minutes, the dough is placed on a 'planc' (round cast-iron griddle) over a clear fire. The planc should not be too hot or the bread will scorch. It is cooked for 20 minutes on each side, then turned, and cooked for another 20 minutes. Fixed gas-fired or electric griddles are now used.

REGION OF PRODUCTION:

South Wales.

Crusty Swansea

DESCRIPTION:

A large round or oval loaf, slashed across the top with 3 diagonal cuts; 200mm diameter, 120–130mm high. Weight: about 800g. Colour and texture: a thick, slightly tough, well-baked crust, gold to dark brown, with a rough, irregular surface; white crumb, fairly close textured with a few irregular large holes.

HISTORY:

According to Christine Gough, who bakes bread in a wood-fired bakehouse at the National Folk Museum, the name 'Swansea' is recognized generally in South Wales for this type of bread. Jan Whitehouse, whose family have been bakers in South Wales for 100 years, states they are simply called 'crusty' loaves in nearby Llanelli. Little is known about their history beyond an oral tradition of long usage. Their shape is closely related to the bloomer loaf, a similar but more elongated crusty, oven-bottom loaf with about eight diagonal cuts on top made in much of southern England. Even the history of this is not well documented. The word may derive from the 'bloom' on the surface or the sheen or lustre of very good quality crumb, or it may relate to the Old English word for ingot (which shape it resembles).

TECHNIQUE:

Although one baker at the Welsh National Folk Museum makes Swanseas according to old-fashioned methods of setting a yeast sponge, the majority are made from conventional white bread dough. After fermentation, the loaves are shaped into ovals, the joins of any folds left on the underside. The cuts in the top crust are made after final proof.

REGION OF PRODUCTION:

South Wales.

Welsh Cake

DESCRIPTION:

A griddle-bread, circular, with deckle edges; about 50–70mm diameter, 10–15mm deep. Weight: 40–50g. Colour: mottled gold brown and cream in large patches, with dried fruit showing through the crust. Flavour and texture: close soft texture, rich flavour.

HISTORY:

Pice ar y maen (Welsh for 'cakes on the stone', where they are also known as *cacennau cri*) have become so well known outside their native area that they are simply termed Welsh cakes. They are a Welsh variant on the theme of flat griddle-breads and scones found throughout western and northern Britain. The recipe now used, leavened with baking powder, cannot date much before the mid-nineteenth century when this ingredient was first introduced. They were known in Glamorgan at the end of that century and they were baked either on a griddle or in a Dutch oven, a three-sided tin oven that was placed directly before the flames of the kitchen fire (Tibbott, 1976). They are still very popular and widely made in their native area. They are cooked on special griddles every day, in full view of the public, by many stallholders in the urban markets of South Wales.

Commercial cakes that use only lard are not as good as those using butter (Freeman, 1980). Cooking on a griddle makes the cakes drier than if they are cooked under a grill or in a Dutch oven. Welsh cakes are very like a Glamorgan variety known as round cakes, and they are not unlike scones, more widely known in the British Isles. They are best eaten hot from the griddle, sprinkled with sugar, or toasted and spread with butter, jam or honey. They are popular for afternoon tea.

TECHNIQUE:

Recipes generally call for flour and fat in the proportions 2:1, with a slightly lower ratio of sugar than fat. A combination of lard and butter or lard and margarine is used. A little sweet spice (cinnamon, allspice and nutmeg) or lemon may be used as a flavouring. The dry ingredients (including leavening) are mixed together, the fat is rubbed in and the mixture is made into a soft dough with egg. Some recipes call for milk. The dough is rolled 5mm thick and cut into rounds with a biscuit cutter. They are cooked on a heated griddle, lightly greased, for 4 minutes each side.

REGION OF PRODUCTION:

Wales, South Wales.

Welsh Pancake

DESCRIPTION:

There are many varieties; in Swansea, circular pancakes are rolled into a long cigar shape; elsewhere, they are left flat; the edges are irregular. Pancakes made in Swansea are 120mm diameter and 7–8mm thick in the middle, thinning slightly towards the edges. Flat pancakes are 120–170mm diameter. A pancake of 120mm diameter weighs about 50g; one of 170mm is 100–125g. Colour: the proportion of white, very lightly cooked batter to pale gold patches, where the pancake has touched the griddle, is variable. In Swansea, white predominates, and the pancakes look smooth; further west they are an even

BROWN AND THE SURFACE IS FULL OF TINY HOLES. WHEN CURRANTS ARE ADDED, THEY ARE INVARIABLY IN A TIGHT CLUSTER IN THE CENTRE OF THE PANCAKE. FLAVOUR AND TEXTURE: VERY LIGHTLY SWEETENED, WITH A SLIGHTLY EGGY FLAVOUR. SOMETIMES LEMON IS ADDED.

HISTORY:

The Celtic cultures of Brittany and Wales have the pancake in common. Wales has long been a stronghold of pancakes – offered for sale in bakeries or on market stalls. Minwel Tibbott (1986) writes that at the beginning of twentieth century, 'the most common luxury item offered for afternoon tea throughout the country would be pancakes or drop scones. The hostess would proceed to bake them after the arrival of an unexpected guest, and they would be served warm, spread liberally with farm butter and homemade jam.' Pancakes were easily made and could be quickly produced. The use of buttermilk for the batter is characteristic, as is a leavening of bicarbonate of soda and vinegar. In this form, the recipe cannot date back beyond the first half of the nineteenth century, when baking soda was first introduced. However, the concept is probably much older. Early recipes contain a high proportion of eggs, although in urban industrial areas, this would have made pancakes into a luxury food.

Each district has its own particular name for the pancake, including: *cramwythen* (Carmarthen/Glamorgan); *crempog* (North Wales); *ffroesen* (Glamorgan); *poncagen* (Pembrokeshire); *pancoesen* (Carmarthen/Cardiganshire). The habit of rolling them up now found in Swansea is a revival of an old custom, other bakers leave pancakes flat. There are many recipes, varying in richness. Welsh pancakes have long been used for savoury foods as well as sweet. For serving, plain pancakes are stacked in layers with a filling of fish or cheese in between, and heated. The stack is cut in quarters to give 4 helpings. Pancakes containing currants are often served with butter and sugar.

TECHNIQUE:

Recipes vary greatly. Milk is the most popular liquid for mixing; buttermilk was traditional. Cream is sometimes cited for special

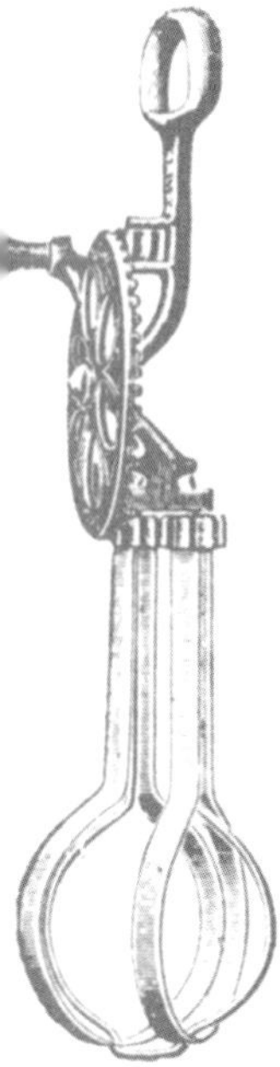

occasions, but it is unlikely that pancakes made with this would be found on sale. One maker, Enfys Marks, uses her grandmother's recipe and finds the use of very fresh milk makes a great difference to the finished result. Margarine often replaces butter in pancakes made for commercial sale. Flour and salt are mixed together in a suitable bowl, melted butter is added, followed by eggs and milk or buttermilk. The mixture is well beaten to make a thin batter, and then left to stand an hour. Some recipes call for a leavening of a little bicarbonate of soda, plus lemon juice or vinegar to be added just before the pancakes are cooked. The batter is beaten again before use. It is cooked in a frying pan or on a griddle until lightly browned on one side, then turned. If currants are added, they are sprinkled on the upper side before turning.

REGION OF PRODUCTION:

Wales.

Welsh Plate Cake

DESCRIPTION:

A flat cake 120mm diameter, 20–30mm thick. Oblong cakes have also been recorded. Weight: about 450g. Colour: pale gold exterior, pale yellow interior, speckled with dried fruit. Flavour and texture: sweet, with a crunchy surface, a moist texture.

HISTORY:

Teisen lap is a Welsh fruit cake. The name means moist cake. Since it was neither friable nor thirst-provoking, it was useful as work-food for coalminers in South Wales (Tibbott, 1976). The recipes must have originally developed from the same sources as other British fruit cakes but there is one very important difference which influenced the final form. It was baked in front of an open fire rather than in an enclosed oven. Until quite recently, *teisen lap* made in Welsh homes was baked in the bottom of a Dutch oven (a 3-sided tin oven that was placed directly before the flames of the kitchen fire), the mixture being either spread on a plate or placed in the shallow oblong pan which forms the base of this utensil. The cake cooked slowly, producing a crunchy surface, now mimicked by sprinkling with sugar and baking in a hot oven. It is possible that 'slab cakes' – wide, shallow, oblong cakes based on a plain sponge mixture containing fat and dried fruit – had their origins in this habit.

TECHNIQUE:

Several recipes exist. They are generally plain with dried fruit. Older versions were mixed with buttermilk; a recipe based on sour cream is also cited by Minwel Tibbott (1976). The version now commonly made calls for flour, butter and sugar in the proportions 4:1:1. Where spices are added, nutmeg is a favourite. The cake is leavened with baking powder.

REGION OF PRODUCTION:

SOUTH WALES.

MENU

The South West

South West England, Channel Islands and Wales

Address Book

Trade Associations and Interest Groups

Asparagus Growers Associaton www.british-asparagus.co.uk
Association of Master Bakers www.masterbakers.co.uk
Association of Scottish Shellfish Growers www.assg.co.uk
Bee Farmers Association www.beefarmers.co.uk
Biscuit, Cake, Chocolate and Confectionary Alliance www.bcca.org.
Bramley Apple Information Service www.bramleyapples.co.uk
Bee Keepers Association www.bbka.org.uk
British Carrot Growers Association www.bcga.info
British Cheese Board www.cheeseboard.co.uk
British Deer Farmers Association www.bdfa.co.uk
British Goose Producers Association www.goose.cc
British Herb Trade Association www.bhta.org.uk
British Pig Association www.britishpigs.co.uk
British Summer Fruits www.britishsummerfruits.co.uk
British Soft Drinks Association www.britishsoftdrinks.com
British Waterfowl Association www.waterfowl.org.uk
Brogdale Horticultural Trust www.brogdale.org
Campaign for Real Ale www.camra.org.uk

Carrot Growers Association www.bcga.info
Common Ground www.england-in-particular.info
Curry Club www.thecurryclub.org.uk
Dairy Trade Federation www.dairyuk.org
English Apples and Pears www.englishapplesandpears.co.uk
English Farm Cider Centre www.middlefarm.com
Food from Britain www.foodfrombritain.co.uk
Food and Drink Federation www.fdf.org.uk
Game Conservancy Trust www.gct.org.uk
Gin and Vodka Association of Great Britain
www.ginvodka.org
Guild of Q Butchers www.guildofqbutchers.com
Henry Doubleday Research Association
(organic gardening and food) www.gardenorganic.org.uk
Herb Society www.herbsociety.co.uk
Kentish Cobnuts Association
www.kentishcobnutsassciation.co.uk
Meat and Livestock Commission www.mlc.org.uk
National Fruit Collection www.webvalley.co.uk
National Association of Cider Makers www.cideruk.com
National Farmers Union www.nfuonline.com
National Federation of Women's Institutes
www.womens-institute.co.uk
National Market Traders Federation www.nmtf.co.uk
National Sheep Association www.nationalsheep.org.uk
Quality Meat Scotland www.qmscotland.co.uk
Rare Breeds Survival Trust www.rbst.org.uk
Sausage Appreciation Society www.sausagefans.com
Scotch Malt Whisky Society www.smws.com
Scottish Association of Master Bakers www.samb.co.uk
Scottish Association of Meat Wholesalers
www.scottish-meat-wholesalers.org.uk
Scottish Crop Research Institute www.scri.sari.ac.uk

Scottish Federation of Meat Traders Association
www.sfmta.co.uk
Scottish Quality Salmon www.scottishsalmon.co.uk
Sea Fish Industry Authority www.seafish.org.uk
Seasoning and Spice Association (UK)
www.seasoningandspice.org.uk
Shellfish Association of Great Britain www.shellfish.org.uk
Soil Association www.soilassociation.org
South-West of England Cider Makers Association
http://tinyurl.com/pylmg
Specialist Cheesemakers Association
www.specialistcheesemakers.co.uk
Taste of Shropshire www.shropshiretourism.info/food-and-drink/
Taste of the West www.tasteofthewest.co.uk
Taste of Wales Ltd www.wela.co.uk
Tastes of Anglia Ltd www.tastesofanglia.com
Three Counties Cider and Perry Association
www.thethreecountiesciderandperryassociation.co.uk
Traditional Farm Fresh Turkey Association
www.golden-promise.co.uk
UK Tea Council www.teacouncil.co.uk
United Kingdom Vineyards Association
www.englishwineproducers.com
Watercress Growers Association www.watercress.co.uk
Wine and Spirit Trade Association www.wsta.co.uk

Producers, Suppliers and Particular Interest Groups

This is by no means an exhaustive list, but this list will point readers wishing to sample a taste of Britain in the right direction. Where possible, a website is given. For smaller organizations or individuals without a functioning website, a postal address is given.

The address book echoes the structure of the text, organized into categories that roughly reflect the natural order of a visit to market: fruit and vegetables, dairy, fishmonger, butchery, bakery, confectioners, drinks and condiments.

Fruit

Dittisham plum

Dittisham Fruit Farm, Capton, Dartmouth, Devon TQ6 0JE.

Vegetables

Jersey Royal potato

Jersey Produce Marketing Organisation www.jerseyroyals.co.uk

Laverbread

Selwyn's Penclawdd Seafoods www.selwynseasfoods.co.uk

Dairy Produce

MILK, CREAM, BUTTER AND ICE CREAM

CHANNEL ISLAND MILK

Quality Milk Producers Ltd, The Bury Farm, Pednor Road, Chesham, Buckinghamshire HP5 2JY.

CLOTTED CREAM BUTTER

R.A. Duckett & Co, Walnut Tree Farm, Heath House, Wedmore, Somerset BS28 4UJ.

CHEESE

BATH CHEESE

Bath soft cheese company www.parkfarm.co.uk

Baydon Hill cheese

J. Hale, Eventide, Baydon Hill Farm, Aldbourne, Wiltshire SN8 2DJ.

BEENLEIGH BLUE CHEESE

Ticklemore Cheese Company, 1 Ticklemore Street, Totnes, Devon TQ9 5EJ.

CAERPHILLY CHEESE

Caws Cenarth Cheese www.cawscenarth.co.uk

Caws Nantybwla Farmhouse Cheese, College Rd, Caermarthen SA31 3QS.

J. Savage, Teif Cheese, Glynhynod Farm, Ffostrasol, Llandysul, Dyfed SA44 5JY.

Trethowan's Dairy Ltd, Gorwydd Farm, Llanddewi Brefi, Tregaron, Ceredigion, Wales SW725 6NY.

R.A. Duckett and Co, Walnut Tree Farm, Heath House, Wedmore, Somerset BS28 4UJ.

CORNISH YARG CHEESE

Lynher Dairies Cheese Company www.cornishyarg.co.uk

CURWORTHY CHEESE

Stockbeare Farm www.curworthycheese.co.uk

Dorset Blue Vinney cheese

The Dorset Blue Soup Company at Woodbridge Farm

www.dorsetblue.com

Double Gloucester cheese

Smart's Traditional Gloucester Cheese www.fmiv.co.uk

C. Martell and Sons, Laurel Farm, Dymock,

Gloucestershire GL18 2DP.

Single Gloucester cheese

Diana Smart, Old Ley Court, Chapel Lane, Birdwood Churcham,

Gloucestershire GL2 8AR.

C. Martell and Sons, Laurel Farm, Dymock,

Gloucestershire GL18 2DP.

Sharpham cheese

M. Sharman www.sharpham.com

Vulscombe cheese

G. Townsend, Higher Vulscombe, Cruwys Morchard,

near Tiverton EX16 8NB.

Fish & Seafood

Cockle (Penclawdd)

The South Wales Sea Fisheries Committee www.swsfc.org.uk

Elvers

The Severn River Authority, Tewkesbury, Gloucestershire.

Smoked mackerel

Andy Race, Fish Merchants Ltd www.andyrace.co.uk

Meat

CATTLE

DEVON CATTLE

The Devon Cattle Breeders Society www.redruby.devon.co.uk

WELSH BLACK CATTLE

The Welsh Black Cattle Society www.welshblackcattlesociety.org

SHEEP

DORSET HORN SHEEP

The Dorset Horn and Poll Sheep Breeders Association
www.dorsetsheep.org

WELSH MOUNTAIN SHEEP

Welsh Lamb and Beef Promotions Ltd.
www.welshlambandbeef.co.uk

PIGS

GLOUCESTERSHIRE OLD SPOTS PIG

Gloucestershire Old Spots Breeders Club www.oldspots.com

SNAILS AND GAME

MENDIP WALLFSH

North Nethercleave Farm & South West Snails
www.south-west-snails.co.uk/devon-farms.htm

Meat Products

Bath chap

Sandridge Farmhouse Bacon www.sandridgefarmhousebacon.co.uk

Farmhouse Fresh Foods, 61 Northgate Street, Gloucester GL1 2AG.

Bradenham ham (Fortnum Black Ham)

Fortnum and Mason www.fortnumandmason.com

Devonshire ham

Heal Farm Meats www.healfarm.co.uk

Glamorgan sausage

Bryson Craske, Abergavenny Fine Foods, Unit 14 Castle Meadows Park, Abergavenny, Gwent NP7 7R2.

Gloucester sausages

The Butts Farm Shop www.thebuttsfarmshop.com

The Gloucester Sausage Company, Unit 1 Knightsbridge Business Centre, Knightsbridge Green, Knightsbridge, Cheltenham, Gloucestershire GL51 9TA.

Welsh bacon

Carmarthen Ham www.carmarthenham.co.uk

Welsh ham

Carmarthen Ham www.carmarthenham.co.uk

Wiltshire bacon

Sandridge Farmhouse Bacon www.sandridgefarmhousebacon.co.uk

Eastbrook Farm Organic Meats www.helenbrowningorganics.co.uk

Breads

Bath bun

Mountstevens Ltd, The Bakery, Fishponds Trading Estate, Clay Hill, Bristol BS5 7ES

Guernsey gâche

L.S. Warry and Sons, PO Box 111, St Peter Port, Guernsey GY1 3EU.

New Senners Bakery, St Martins, Guernsey.

Sally Lunn

The Sally Lunn Shop www.sallylunns.co.uk

Griddle-breads, biscuits & Puddings

Cornish fairings

Furniss of Cornwall www.furniss-foods.co.uk

Cakes & Pies

Apple cake

Mrs M. Stewart, Lower Farmhouse, Sandford Orchas, Sherborne, Dorset.

Dorset knobs

Moores www.moores-biscuits.co.uk

Welsh plate cake

Miss E. Marks, Popty Bach-y-Wlad, Court Farm, Pentrecourt, Llandyssul, Dyfed.

Aromatics & Condiments

Tewkesbury mustard

Kitchen Garden Preserves www.kitchengardenpreserves.co.uk

Urchfont mustard

The Tracklement Co Ltd www.tracklements.co.uk

Beverages

Cider (West Country)

The Hereford Cider Museum www.cidermuseum.co.uk

John Hallam, 27 Fraser Street, Windmill Hill, Bedminster, Bristol BS3 4LZ.

H. Weston and Sons, The Bounds, Much Marcle, Herefordshire HR8 2NQ.

Plymouth gin

The Blackfriars Distillery www.plymouthgin.com

[illegible]

Allied Domecq http://allieddomecq.com

PGOs and PGIs

Britain and continental Europe possess an enormous range of wonderful food. When a product's reputation extends beyond national borders, however, it can find itself in competition with products using the same name and passing themselves off as genuine. This unfair competition discourages producers and misleads consumers, and for this reason the European Union in 1992 created systems known as Protected Designation of Origin and Protected Geographical Indication to promote and protect regionally important food products. A Protected Designation of Origin (PDO) describes a food that is produced, processed and prepared in a given geographical area, using a recognised skill. A Protected Geographical Indication (PGI) demonstrates a geographical link between a foodstuff and a specific region in at least one of the stages of production, processing or preparation.

For more information, visit
http://ec.europa.eu/agriculture/qual/en/uk_en.htm

Bibliography

Unless otherwise indicated, the place of publication is London and the country of publication is the United Kingdom.

Acton, Eliza (1845), *Modern Cookery for Private Families,* facsimile ed., introduction by Elizabeth Ray, 1993, Southover Press, Lewes.

Austen, Jane (1995), *Jane Austen's Letters,* ed. D. Le Faye, Oxford.

Beeton, Isabella (1861), *Beeton's Book of Household Management*, facsimile ed. 1982, Chancellor Press.

Black, M. (1989), *Paxton and Whitfeld's Fine Cheese*, Little Brown.

Borrow, George (1862), *Wild Wales.*

Boyd, Lizzie (1976), *British Cookery*, Croom Helm, Bromley.

Bradley, Martha (1756), *The British Housewife*, facsimile ed. 1997-8, Prospect Books, Totnes.

Brears, P. (1984), *The Gentlewoman's Kitchen*, Wakefeld Historical Publications, Wakefeld.

——— (1998), *The Old Devon Farmhouse*, Devon Books, Tiverton.

British Medical Association, (c. 1950), 'All about Tripe', Family Doctor Magazine.

Brown, M. (1986), 'Cider Making in the Channel Isles', Folk Life, vol. 25.

Cassell's (1896), *Cassell's Dictionary of Cookery* (first ed. c. 1875).

Cheke, V. (1959), *The Story of Cheesemaking in Britain*, Routledge and Kegan Paul.

Cox, J. Stevens (1971), *Guernsey Dishes of Bygone Days, St Peter Port*, Guernsey.

Dallas, E.S. (1877), *Kettner's Book of The Table*, facsimile ed.1968, Centaur Press.

David, Elizabeth(1977), *English Bread and Yeast Cookery*, Allen Lane.

Davidson, Alan E. (1979) *North Atlantic Seafood*, Macmillan.

——— (1988) *Seafood, A Connoisseur's Guide and Cookbook*, Mitchell Beazley.

——— (1991), *Fruit*, Mitchell Beazley.

——— (1993) 'Sherbets', Liquid Nourishment, ed. C.A. Wilson, Edinburgh University Press.

Davies, S. (1993), 'Vinetum Britannicum, Cider and Perry in the seventeenth century', *Liquid Nourishment*, ed. C.A. Wilson, Edinburgh University Press.

'Dods, Meg' ['Dods, Mrs Margaret, of the Cleikum Inn, St Ronan's'] (1826), *The Cook and House-wife's Manual*, Edinburgh. (Written anonymously by Christian Isobel Johnstone.)
Evans, J. (1994), *The Good Beer Guide* (1995), CAMRA Books, St Albans.
Farley, John (1783), *The London Art of Cookery*.
FitzGibbon, Theodora (1965), *The Art of British Cooking*, Phoenix House.
——— (1972), *A Taste of England, The West Country*, Dent.
Freeman, Bobby (1980), *First Catch Your Peacock*, Image Imprint, Grifffthstown.
French, R.K. (1982), *The History and Virtues of Cyder*, Robert Hale.
Fussell, G.E. (1966), *The English Dairy Farmer 1500–1900*, Frank Cass and Co Ltd.
Glasse, Hannah (1747), *The Art of Cookery Made Plain and Easy*, facsimile 1983, Prospect Books.
Green, Henrietta (1993), *Food Lover's Guide to Britain*, BBC Books.
Grigson, Jane(1984), *Observer Guide to British Cookery*, Michael Joseph.
Hall, S.J.G. and Clutton-Brock, J. (1989), *Two Hundred Years of British Farm Livestock*, British Museum.
Hartley, Dorothy (1954), *Food in England*, Macdonald and Janes.
Henderson, W.A. (c. 1790), *The Housekeeper's Instructor*.
Hogan, W. (1978), *The Complete Book of Bacon*, Northwood Publications.
Irons, J.R. (c. 1935), *Breadcraft*, privately published.
Jenkins, J,G. (1971), 'Commercial Salmon Fishing in Welsh Rivers', Folk Life, vol. 9.
——— (1977), 'Cockles and Mussels, aspects of shellfsh gathering in South Wales', Folk Life, vol. 15.
Kirkland, J. (1907), *The Modern Baker, Confectioner and Caterer*, Gresham Publishing Company.
Kitchiner, W. (1817), *The Cook's Oracle* (1829 ed.). Larousse Gastronomique (1938), Paris.
Mabey, David (1978), *In Search of Food, traditional eating and drinking in Britain*, Macdonald and Jane's.
Marshall, Mrs A.B. (1887), *Mrs A.B. Marshall's Cookery Book*, 1st ed. (n.d.)
Martin, C. (1993), *Our Daily Bread*, Tabb House, Padstow.
Merrick, Heather (1990), *Pasties and Cream*, Helston.
Morgan, Joan and Richards, Alison (1993), *A Book of Apples*, Ebury Press.
Murrell, John (1638), *Murrels Two books of Cookerie and Carving 1638*, facsimile ed.1985, Jackson's of Ilkley.
Nott, J. (1726), *Cook's and Confectioner's Dictionary*, facsimile ed. 1980, Lawrence Rivington.
Penrose, John (1983), *Letters from Bath*, 1766–1767, ed.
Raffael, Michael(1997), *West Country Cooking, Baking*, Halsgrove, Tiverton.

Raffald, E. (1769), *The Experienced English Housekeeper*, facsimile of 1782 ed. 1970, E&W Books.
Rance, Patrick (1982), *The Great British Cheese Book*, Macmillan.
[Rundell, Maria Eliza] (1807), *A New System of Domestic Cookery*, by a Lady.
Schnebbelie, J.C. (1804), *The Housekeeper's Instructor* by W.A. Henderson, corrected revised and considerably improved by Jacob Christopher Schnebbelie.
Simon, A.L. (1960), *The Concise Encyclopaedia of Gastronomy*, Collins (1983 ed., Penguin Books).
Skuse, E. (c. 1892), *The Confectioner's Handbook.*
Spicer, D.G. (1949), *From an English Oven*, The Women's Press, New York, USA.
Stobart, Tom (1980), *The Cook's Encyclopaedia*, Batsford.
Thompson, Flora (1939), *Lark Rise to Candleford*, Guild Books.
Tibbott, Minwel (1976), *Welsh Fare*, The National Museum of Wales, Cardiff.
Tusser, Thomas (1573), *Five Hundred Points of Good Husbandry*, 1984 ed., Oxford University Press.
Webb, Mrs A. (c. 1930), *Farmhouse Cookery*, George Newnes.
White, Florence (1932), *Good Things in England*, Jonathan Cape.
Wilson, C. Anne (1973), *Food and Drink in Britain*, Constable.
Woolgar, V.M. (1992), *Household Accounts from Medieval England*, 2 vols, The British Academy.
Wright, Joseph (1896–1905), *The English Dialect Dictionary*, Henry Frowde.
Youatt, W. (1834), *Cattle.*

Acknowledgements

South West, Channel Islands, Wales

From Bath Chaps to Bara Brith

The Taste of South West Britain

Particular thanks to the following chefs, authors and journalists who generously contributed pieces to the book:

John Burton Race (p.27), Matthew Fort (p.47), Mark Hix (p.97).

The following people have kindly given the compilers information about particular foods and trades. This book could not have been completed without their assistance.

A. Beer, Barnstaple, Devon; G. Chubb, Taunton, Somerset; G. Davies, Cardiff, South Wales; A. de Gruchy, St Mary's, Jersey; T. Evans, Barnstaple, Devon; Trevor Fawcett, Bath; M. French, Langport, Somerset; W. Gosling, Swindon, Wiltshire; C. Gough, Cardiff, South Wales; J. Griffths, Denbigh, North Wales; J. Hale, Aldbourne, Wiltshire; D. Hall, Bristol; R. Hayes, Bristol; N. Johns, Bristol; B. Jones, Penclawdd, South Wales; R. Keen, Chippenham, Wiltshire; B. Lake, Launceston, Cornwall; P. Lawson, Cornwall; R. Lutwyche, Cirencester, Gloucestershire; B. Matthews, Crediton, Devon; K. Mold, Bangor, North Wales; A. Muller, The Lizard, Cornwall; G. Padfeld, Bath; D. Payne, Plymouth, Devon; A. Petch, Heal's Farm, Devon; N. Pooley, Chewton Mendip, Somerset; N. Pugh, Pembrokeshire; A. Rees, Carmarthen, Dyfed; R. Reynolds, Priddy, Somerset; D. Rossiter, Kingsbridge, Devon; Dr Scofeld, Cardiff; D. Smart, Churcham, Gloucestershire; J. Temperley, Kingsbury Episcopi, Somerset; D. Thomas, Aberystwyth; M. Tibbot, Cardiff; G. Townsend, Tiverton, Devon; J. Tullberg, Malmesbury, Wiltshire; J. Whitehouse, Swansea, South Wales; J. Williams, Bristol.